Prominent Sociologists Since World War II

Don Albert Martindale

University of Minnesota

CHARLES E. MERRILL PUBLISHING COMPANY
A Bell & Howell Company
Columbus, Ohio

Published by
Charles E. Merrill Publishing Company
A Bell & Howell Company
Columbus, Ohio 43216

ISBN: 0-675-08795-3

Library of Congress Catalog Card Number: 74-76125

1 2 3 4 5 6 7 — 80 79 78 77 76 75 74

Printed in the United States of America

For

Lowry and Florence Nelson

Preface

By circumstances of its origin, as the last born of traditional Western   23
philosophy, sociology has been destined to struggle with all the old
conundrums. Inevitably the various alternative approaches to these
problems have been the starting points for distinct sociological formulations.

One of the important questions facing the sociological theorist is   27
the source of the diverse points of view and of the trends and movements in sociological theory. With special frequency his attempt to
answer these questions takes him back to the forms and problems of
philosophy. Often the originators of sociological theories were powerful figures who found the way to establish the sociological relevance of philosophic points of view and issues.

The more firmly established a science, the more completely it   33
becomes a discipline dominated by its theory rather than its theorists. Sociology has not yet fully passed beyond the heroic stage of its
development. Many of its most interesting formulations still bear the
personal imprint of the founders. In the long run the personality of
its originator and the circumstances of its origin are irrelevant to a
scientific theory. It is acceptable to approach theory in this manner
only so long as it explains the subject matter better than its alternatives.

However, the theories that first dominate a science continue to influence it in an established manner, drawing others along their course. These first theories aid in investigation of some matters and hamper the investigation of others. A science, in fact, may never completely lose its character as a historically unique development. One value of inquiring into individual biographical and historical factors which shaped the rise and development of a science is to advance one's understanding of the points where the historical aspect of the discipline must be differentiated from its scientifically established features.

The ideas of a science are always and only the inventions of individuals. Hence, particularly in the dawn period of the discipline, this question is always of interest: what led a given individual at some given time and place to his formulations; what in turn in the *milieu* accounts for their reception? The examination of the interaction of personality and *milieu*, particularly of the charismatic heroes of the discipline, is the only reasonable way to isolate individual psychological and historical factors of the discipline. It goes without saying that the validity of the theories of the charismatic heroes of the discipline is often quite another matter from the question of what led to their formulations, and why these formulations were accepted.

In the present volume the influence of personality and *milieu* upon theoretical formulations will be illustrated for Max Weber, C. Wright Mills, Talcott Parsons, and Pitirim A. Sorokin. Max Weber has been estimated by some thinkers to have been the greatest sociologist of all time. Talcott Parsons and C. Wright Mills are of interest, for in the post-World War II period they have moved to positions of dominance, polarizing the field between them until the untimely death of C. Wright Mills.

Finally, the intellectual biography of Pitirim A. Sorokin is of interest because of various anomalies in his career. Perhaps more than any other person, Sorokin could until the time of his death legitimately claim to be the foremost sociologist in the contemporary world. As far as it has been possible to determine, his works have been translated into more languages than any other sociologist who ever lived. Yet Sorokin never founded a school or a movement.

Max Weber, C. Wright Mills, Talcott Parsons, and Pitirim A. Sorokin reveal in their careers and writings some of the forms of influence of the personality of its heroes on the historical shape of sociology.

Acknowledgments

The author would like to thank the following:

Dissent for permission to reprint excerpts from "C. Wright Mills: A Personal Memoir" by Harvey Swados, *Dissent* X, 1 (Winter 1963).

The New York Times for excerpts from "A Mentor of Sociologists Retires After 42 Years at Harvard Post" by Robert Reinhold, *The New York Times*, 14 June 1973. © 1973 by The New York Times Company. Reprinted by permission.

Helen P. Sorokin for permission to reprint excerpts from "Similarities and Dissimilarities Between Two Sociological Systems" by Pitirim A. Sorokin, mimeographed.

College and University Press for permission to reprint excerpts from *A Long Journey* by Pitirim A. Sorokin (New Haven, Conn.: College and University Press, 1963).

The Sociological Quarterly for permission to reprint excerpts from "Politics and Social Structure" by Don Martindale, *The Sociological Quarterly*, Summer 1970, pp. 416–18.

Contents

ix

The Birth of Sociology from the Spirit of Philosophy

In Western cultural development, the philosophy of old represented the romance and heroism of the mind, being the adventures of intrepid warriors on their long journeys home from the wars. The heroic phase of Western thought is, perhaps, at an end, for the distinctive movements in Western philosophy in the twentieth century, analytical philosophy and existentialism, have, each in its own way, been opposed to the main course of traditional Western thought.

Analytical philosphy has inclined toward extreme positivism or radical empiricism and in the name of an often narrowly conceived methodological rationalism has rejected much of the traditional heritage of philosphy as pure verbalism. Extentialism, at the opposite pole, has sharply questioned the rationalistic traditions of Western thought and has sought consolation in nonrational features of individual mental processes. In different ways both movements have shown a conviction that Western philosphy in its traditional sense is no longer viable.

The Spirit of Western Philosophy

By the spirt of Western philosophy is meant the set of attitudes and ideals which have made it the great founder of disciplines. This spirit

1

has been characterized by uninhibited curiosity and an aspiration to an understanding of every mystery of man and nature. Fundamental to its ethos is the assumption that the quest for ultimate knowledge is a legitimate individual activity and an achievement lying within the powers of the average mind. The spirit of Western philosophy recognized no forbidden fruit on the tree of knowledge.

Philosophy's role as the great founder of disciplines in the West has been inseparable from this spirit of irreverence or impiety which has acknowledged no forbidden areas or taboo spheres of the mind reserved to the gods and their interpreters. It also has been rather anarchistic, since it assigns no priority to any position simply because it may enjoy collective support. It has been revolutionary for it acknowledges no necessary association between the human condition and truth, hence no intellectual controversy can be settled by institutional authority.

The spirit of Western philosophy has not enjoyed continuous or unchanged reception from classical Greek days. It has been intermittent, displaying distinct forms in the ancient and modern worlds.

The Classical Temper

There is no conceivable way of preventing a creature who has once transformed the circumstances of his life by tools and language from exploring the world in ever-widening circles and dreaming of solving all its problems. However, it is also true that man's capacity to pose problems considerably outruns his capacity to solve them.

Language introduces into immediate experience factors and considerations that are not physically present. By means of language men are able to set up plans of action the execution of which lies days, months, or even years away, radically transforming the temporal dimensions of experience. Language makes it possible to review the past for its bearing on the present and to introduce into the experience of one man the results of the experiences of others remote in time and space. The experience of a language-using creature, in short, is always to some extent in response to things outside the immediate situation.

This continuous responsiveness of linguistic structured experience to non-present, perhaps even nonexistent, possibilities also saddles man with problems outside the scope of other animals. Man is even able to contemplate and accommodate himself to the possibility of his own death. He inquires into the origins and destinies not only of himself but of mankind, of possible life on other worlds, of the origin and destruction of the very universe. On joyous occasions he may be plunged into melancholy by his sense of transience; in times of adversity he may be exalted to heights of ecstacy by his hopes.

At times the introduction of the possible into the sphere of the actual not only provides human behavior with unusual effectiveness but adds a new category of risk. Unless control is exercised over the endlessly varied alternatives the human mind casts up around every course of action, no collective task can be carried through. Unless closure is achieved with respect to the questions the human mind raises, man's resolve is disspirited by Hamlet-like doubts. An age-old function of magic and religion is to bring emotional and conceptual closure with respect to many of the matters falling outside the effectiveness of workaday routines.

Magic and religion, among other things, institute a system of controls in the world of possibilities. Wherever magic and religion are vital they curtail the free movement of man's intelligence. In part this is their purpose. Philosophy can arise only under circumstances where magical taboos are losing their power and where the religious closure of ideas is ceasing to be effective. In other words, the priestly monopoly of things of the spirit had to be broken and sacred areas opened for secular investigaton for philosophy to appear.

In the first millenium B.C. in a number of the centers of civilization, conditions favored the emergence of a stratum of educated men familiar with the lore of the priests but with sufficient independence to choose freely between the available religious doctrines or even to reject them.

In ancient India during the same period when various leaders of heterodox sections, Gautama (Buddhism), Mahavira (Jainism), and Gosala (The Ajivikas sect), were ignoring the traditional Hindu gods in their religious teachings, a fluid intellectual situation had developed which permitted some educated individuals to turn their backs on religion altogether. The circumstances which conspired to produce this result are of interest.

In the second millenium B.C. a city civilization had begun to flourish in the river valleys of Northern India. Toward the end of the epoch a warlike cattle-breeding people pushed into India from the northeast, violently destroying the cities along their path. The cities which had passed their prime did not seem capable of defending themselves against the primitives. The chariot-building cattle breeders spread as a thin stratum of conquerors over a large native population. They preferred their individual house chaplains to the communal priests of the native tribes. Like their Homeric counterparts, these house chaplains sang the praises of the gods and heroes; they presided over sacrifices and other ceremonial practices of the eminent households they served. They evolved into bearers of an extensive heroic and religious literature. They also served as tutors to the children of the household, primarily in religious lore but secondarily in other knowledge and skills required by their patrons.[1] The priest singers and their descendants thus came to monopolize much of the intellectual culture of their societies.

In time, as the conquerors spread down over northern India, they ceased in their turn to be an exclusively rural, semifeudal stratum. They engaged in brisk trade and commerce, formed city communities, and consolidated kingdoms. Particularly in the capital cities aggregations of people arose and formed strata whose religious and intellectual needs fell outside the sphere of competence of the old type of house priest. Educated upper strata, who were bearers of intellectual culture, emerged outside the ranks of the priesthood. From their ranks new religious formations proceeded along with a self-consciously antireligious philosophy.

The earliest identifiable teacher of an antireligious philosophy in India was Ajita Keśakambalin whose views had many similarities to those of the classical Greek atomists. Man, Ajita theorized, is composed of four elements: earth, water, fire, and air. Man's peculiarity depends on how these elements are arranged. When he dies, this arrangement is destroyed; nothing survives.

> When he dies earth returns to the aggregate of earth, water to water, fire to fire, and air to air, while his senses vanish into space. Four men with the bier take up the corpse; they gossip [about the dead man] as far as the burning-ground, where his bones turn the colour of a dove's wing and his sacrifices end in ashes. They are fools who preach almsgiving, and those who maintain the existence [of immaterial categories] speak vain and lying nonsense. When the body dies both fool and wise man alike are cut off and perish. They do not survive after death.[2]

Ajita formed the center of a cultivated circle which Basham compares to the Epicureans of classical Greece.

Indian materialism, variously called Carvakas or Lokayatas, was convinced that all forms of religious belief were mythology or humbug. Many of its proponents believed that the guiding forces of life were pleasure and pain, suggesting that, like the utilitarians of the West, they were empirically inclined and consulted their own experiences for the interpretations of that experience. While opponents to Indian materialism denied any ethical positions, there are many indirect suggestions that they advanced ethical positions similar to those of the Epicureans of antiquity or the utilitarians of modern times.

While most that is known about the position can only be gleaned from the writings of its opponents, materialism never completely disappeared from Indian thought. From the ninth century survives a philosophical work known as *The Tartvopaplavasimha* by Jayarasi which with considerable dialectical skill seeks to destroy the basic presuppositions of the chief religious systems of the time.

However, while India sustained the rise of a secular philosophy, it was thrust into the background to function primarily as a secular critique of religious outlooks.

In ancient China, too, conditions favored the emergence of a philosophic outlook. In his study of Chinese philosophy Fung Yu-lan describes philosophy as "systematic, reflective thinking on life."[3] Religion, too, he observes, has something to do with life. In fact, "in the heart of every great religion there is a philosophy . . . with a certain amount of superstructure, which consists of superstitions, dogmas, rituals, and institutions."[4] However, philosophy proper, as Fung sees it, is systematic reflection about the problems of life freed from such religious wrappings.

In ancient China a philosophic outlook in this sense came to dominate the cultivated mind. Confucianism, its dominant tradition, became so pervasive in traditional China as to lead many Western interpreters to compare it to religion. Confucianism's *Four Books* became a virtual Bible of the Chinese people. However, as a system of thought Confucianism is more comparable to Platonism or Aristotelianism than to Christian theology. The *Four Books* lack the kinds of materials particularly identified with religion in the West; there is no story of creation, no concept of life in the beyond, no notion of heaven or hell. Beside Confucianism two other systems of belief flourished in ancient China: Taoism and Buddhism. Taoism, which was native to China, and Buddhism, which anciently migrated from India, were subject to the Chinese impetus toward philosophy, though both have associated religions.

Taoistic philosophy is called *Tao chia* and is distinct from Taoist religion (*Tao chiao*). Similarly, Buddhist philosophy, *Fo hsueh*, is distinct from Buddhist religion, *Fo chiao*. Fung Yu-lan observes that "to the educated Chinese, Buddhist philosophy is more interesting than the Buddhist religion."[5] In ancient China philosophy came to occupy a place comparable to religion in the Occident, leading Fung Yu-lan to conclude that the Chinese "are not religious because they are philosophical."[6]

The events which thrust religion of a Western type aside in ancient China and which ensconced a philosophic orientation in its place were roughly as follows: In the second millennium the Chinese high cultural area was dominated by a city civilization in which a typical ancient city religion (with sky gods, priestly hierarchies, temples, sacrifices, and so on) dominated intellectual life. When this city civilization was replaced by a feudal system the monopoly on intellectual life by a literate priestly hierarchy was broken. In place of the former city cult, a vigorous growth of household cults (the cult of ancestors) occurred. However, the stratum of educated men did not disappear. As experts on ceremonies and as persons possessing literary and administrative skills, the stratum of literate individuals found employment in administrative centers of the feudal kingdoms. However, the role of this stratum of educated men had ceased to be primarily religious. Nor were they any longer trained in priest-dominated, temple-domiciled schools. They transmitted their skills to apprentices and, in time, organized private schools of their own. The mandarin intellectuals of China's feudal period were destined by their situation to devote their talents to man's social destiny apart from any special religious commitments.[7] Such intellectuals often migrated from one state to another, serving in a variety of administrative capacities and acquiring a broad comparative knowledge of political, administrative, and social problems.

Between 480 and 222 B.C., the period of Warring States, a series of elimination contests between rival feudal states began to reduce their number. Eventually the state of Ch'in gained supremacy and succeeded in unifying the entire cultural area. This conquest and consolidation marked the transformation of ancient China from a crude shifting hegemony of feudal states to an empire. The status of the mandarin intellectual also was transformed. He ceased to be a free-lance intellectual and feudal retainer, becoming instead a bureaucratic official qualified for his post by passing state-directed civil service examinations. If anything, however, his character as a secular intellectual was emphasized by the change.

As under its feudal states, the economy of imperial China remained primarily agricultural, perhaps more than under the late stages of feudalism when city communities had begun to flourish. The critical economic difference between the two periods was the decline of feudal types of manorial enterprise and the rise in importance of the economy of the peasant household. Religion remained primarily an affair of the household.

The two major impulses in Chinese thought, Taoism and Confucianism, "are poles apart from one another, yet they are also the two poles of one and the same axis. They both express, in one way or another, the aspirations and inspirations of the farmer."[8] The Taoists idealized the simplicity of primitive society and condemned civilization. They also idealized the innocence of children and despised knowledge. . . . They made a sharp distinction between what is of nature and what is of man, the natural and the artificial. According to them, what is of nature is the source of human happiness and what is of man is the root of all human suffering.[9]

The Confucians, on the other hand, fashioned their theories around the traditional family system. Of the five social relationships which the Confucians made central to their system (between sovereign and subject, father and son, elder and younger brothers, husband and wife, friend and friend) three are from the family. The ancestor worship of a family centered on the founder of the family who symbolized its unity in a manner indispensable for a large complex organization. "A great part of Confucianism," Fung Yu-lan maintains, "is the rational justification of this social system or its theoretical expression. Economic conditions prepared its basis and Confucianism expressed its ethical significance."[10]

While Chinese philosophic orientations achieved a diffusion of a comprehensiveness rarely approached in the West, they remained tied to specific social relationships much more closely.

In classical Greece in the same general time period that the philosophic outlook appeared in India and China, philosophy achieved its most developed form. The bearers of the philosophic outlook were citizen-soldiers of the Mediterranean sea cities.

The oldest of such sea cities represented communities of a new type formed around what had originally been castles of feudal lords of the Greek Heroic period. From such castles the feudal lords supervised the agricultural work that sustained them and launched piratical expeditions in the eastern Mediterranean, adding booty and slaves to their household economies. In time these pirates began to run out of places to raid and began to depend less on raiding and more on peaceful trade. However, warfare for plunder remained a feature of the ancient sea cities to the latest period, as earlier it had for the castles that preceded them. Moreover, as raiding expeditions declined, the warrior companions of the nobles who had participated as share partners insisted upon rights of participation in the opportunities for trade.

One could, perhaps, date the origins of the ancient city-state from the time when aristocracies began to replace the kings in control of various sea fortresses. Many cities (such as Athens and Sparta) in historical times commemorated a day on which the synoecism of the city had occurred. It was usual for revolutionary nobles who took the affairs of these fortress centers into their hands to establish a religious cult of the city over and beyond the cults of their respective households. The ancient city, thus, was in some measure a religious community as well as a warrior community; its temple (the house of the city god) was also its treasury. The temple was not a place for congregational worship so much as a house of the city god. The full citizens of the city were warrior politicians who also participated as equals in the Olympian cults.

While the oldest of such cities were established by revolutionary uprisings of nobles against the feudal kings of the late Heroic period, once the new city-states became going concerns, cities were often founded by colonies sent out from a mother city. Such daughter cities rapidly became autonomous, usually losing all ties except those of sentiment and economic advantage with the founding city.

To the latest period of the free city-state of Western antiquity, the economy of the city rested on war as well as on trade. Wars were followed by distribution of slaves and booty. Citizenship was jealously guarded for its rights of participation in the spoils of war as well as its other privileges. As time went by the wars of the Greek city-states had few other opponents than each other.

In the course of their incessant wars the Greek city-states became bearers of the most developed forms of military technology of the day. Increasing reliance began to be placed on the disciplined foot soldier (rather than on the horse-drawn chariot and individual knight) on land and on the free sailor (in contrast to the slave oarsman) at sea. In the Persian wars the unexpected victory of the city-states confirmed these military institutions which evolved rapidly thereafter. As the military base of the city widened, so, too, did the base of its citizenship. The partial democratization of warfare was accompanied by a partial democratization of the city. The Olympian city cults were changed in the process. Aristocratic priesthoods were thrust into the background, and religious office was increasingly democratized. In time in some cities (Athens) many of the lower religious offices were filled by drawing lots.

The distinctive activities of the ancient citizen were warfare and politics. He trained constantly for hand-to-hand combat in the gymnasium which was one of the distinctive institutions of the *polis.* He argued politics in the forum. He derived much of his livelihood from war plunder and the productivity of slaves who were primarily secured as booty. However, he also constantly ran the risk, should his city lose a war, of being pressed into slavery himself.

No one has seen more clearly than Max Weber the extent to which the life of the civilian soldier of the ancient city-state was stylized in terms of the activity which established his status: hand-to-hand combat. From early times, Weber observed, in the city-state the warrior had begun to test and develop his military fitness by wrestling in the ring. As hand-to-hand combat moved to the forefront of the military technology of the ancient world, this training of naked warriors became the symbol of their uniqueness. All events of the gymnasium (spear throwing, foot racing, wrestling, disc throwing) began to assume the form of contests with referees under specific rules for prizes. From the contest of naked warriors training for war, the idea diffused to all other spheres. Official festivals increasingly took the form of occasions for contests of many sorts: dramatic contests, athletic contests, song contests. From the gymnasium the concept of the contest diffused to the whole of life until "alongside the Epics it became the single most important bond of the Hellenic world in contrast to all barbarians."[11]

Classical Greek artists had an unprecedented opportunity to observe the naked body of the trained athlete brought to a state of physical perfection by years in the gymnasium. The forms of naked bodies of contesting warriors dominated the plastic and graphic arts. The ritualistic song of honor to the gods took the form of a musical contest. Political issues were settled in oratorical contests. Even the preferred form of the philosophic reasoning became the verbal contest or dialogue. Philosophers such as Plato and Aristotle took their models from the orators in a manner comparable to the way the artists took their models from contesting warriors.

The distinctive properties of the classical temper of Western philosophy emerged under these circumstances. The citizen soldier was used to seeing his problems as a whole for which he was individually responsible. Religion supplied no basis for settling disputes, since he and his peers were comembers of the city cult, sharing at least minor religious positions in the same manner that they shared military and political responsibilities and privileges. The ancient citizen's thought was not that of a feudal retainer or of a bureaucrat who presupposed the existence of one or other sort of grade hierarchy. Nor was his thought, as in India, that of a secular moralist standing over and against the priesthood. He was an amateur, a democratic participant in his city community who could, potentially, hold any given position in it. Just as he settled questions of military competence in hand-to-hand contests and political questions by debate, he sought to settle all speculative questions by an idealized contest represented by his philosophic dialogue. Methodology, thus, was one of his primary concerns.

The classical temper of Western philosophy rested on the presuppositions of wholeness, rationality, formal symmetry, and the need for methodological clarity.

The Modern Temper

When the ancient city lost its autonomy the classical spirit flickered and died. The time was to come when the highest intellectual types of the Western world would be religious figures once more. Even the products of the ancient philosophers were no longer read, and many were lost.

In the cities that emerged in the Western Middle Ages conditions once more appeared favorable to the rise of speculative secular thought apart from religious contents. The spirit of philosophy was re-born in a new form. Many equivalent conditions as well as important differences to those of the classical city-state were present. Religion, for example, took quite a different form from the formation of city cults of ancient times.

Christianity had survived the early Middle Ages in part by retreating into monastic communities, in part by being feudalized. Many of the new cities arose at the sites of episcopal sees which had been established in Roman cities when Christianity was made into the official religion of the Empire. The decline of urban life had left the bishops in the position of administrative and religious heads of essentially rural districts. The bishops were often feudalized. In the late tenth and early eleventh centuries new aggregations of traders and craftsmen began to collect at many of the sites of the old Roman cities. When they put pressure on the bishops for local autonomy, the bishops often regarded this as a threat and resisted it. A number of revolutions against the authority of the bishops resulted. Later such rights were often granted without the necessity of revolutionary uprisings.

The fact that in the early states of city formation revolutionary uprisings occurred against church authority is testimony enough of the fact that the city communities contained conditions which promoted the rise of secular intellectuality. However, the members of the new urban communities were not necessarily irreligious; they merely wanted a religion adapted to their needs. They often took matters into their own hands and formed a variety of associations for religious and other purposes (funerals, celebrations, religious ceremonies, protection, care for widows and orphans). In such associations a state of religious equality existed which neutralized religion as a basis for settling problems in somewhat the same manner as was true for members of the religious cult of the ancient *polis.*

Moreover, in the cities a variety of new avenues was opened for social, economic, and political mobility for which traditional religious forms had little relevance. Men were cast upon their personal resources for the invention of new social forms and the accommodation to experiences that fell outside the compass of traditional institutions. They often discovered that the literatures from antiquity were more relevant than church writings.

While there were many points of similarity between the medieval and ancient city which invited a comparable development of secular intellectuality, there were also significant contrasts which tended to give it quite a new form. The medieval city was a community of merchants, artisans, and artists, not of warriors. In the ancient city the merchant was often a foreigner (a *metic*), and the artisan often a slave. Slave labor tended to fix the standing of the ancient laborer; the medieval city rested on free labor. The medieval city occasionally had its city militia or hired mercenary armies, but it was not the bearer of the most advanced military technology of the time. Moreover, the city association was much more comprehensive, while the ancient city was in the hands of a restricted clique.

The medieval urbanite had a progressive attitude toward materials and technology in contrast to his ancient counterpart. He was more inclined to seek the answer to his conceptual problems by research of the literature of the past than by means of Socratic dialogues. His solutions to practical problems rested on trial and error which at times approached experimentalism. The methodologies of the medieval urbanite (scholarly research in intellectual problems and experimentalism in practical problems) played only a minor role in the ancient world.

The classic temper had its point of gravity in the rationality of the civilian soldier; the modern temper had its point of gravity in the taste and judgment of the artist-scholar. The typical philosophic work of the classic period was the dialogue; that of the modern period was the essay, the literary work of art.

The combined effect of the classic and modern tempers sent Western thought on a course distinct from that of other world areas where philosophic thinking also appeared. In India much of the speculative thought on ultimate questions which in the West occurred in philosophic contexts remained permanently within the confines of religion. Moreover, while a refined methodological consciousness developed in India, it was in the service of religious disputation. Philosophy proper always fought a rear guard action against religion in India.

In China the same conditions that led to an unusually broad diffusion of a philosophic outlook also played a major role in restricting its scope. The bearers of Chinese philosophy were primarily intermediate officials, first under various feudal administrations, later under the Empire. Chinese philosophy reflected the point of view and responsibilities of such officials. In Fung Yu-lan's words:

> Chinese philosophy, regardless of its different schools of thought, is directly or indirectly concerned with government and ethics. On the surface, therefore, it is concerned chiefly with society, and not with the universe; with the daily functions of human relations, not hell and heaven; with man's present life, but not his life in a world to come. When he was once asked by a disciple about the meaning of death, Confucius replied: "Not yet understanding life, how can you understand death?" (*Analects*, XI, ll.) And Mencius said: "The sage is the acme of human relations." (Mencius, IVa, 2), which, taken literally, means that the sage is the morally perfect man in society.[12]

The self-conscious task of the mandarin intellectual was to make the traditional order of China work. The typical philosopher occupied a position that made him practically as well as conceptually responsible for the stability of his society. As a result, in Professor Y. L. Chin's words:

> Chinese philosophers were all of them different grades of Socrates. This was so because ethics, politics, reflective thinking, and knowledge were unified in the philosopher; in him, knowledge and virtue were one and inseparable. His philosophy required that he live it; he was himself its vehicle.[13]

The development of speculative possibilities in abstraction from life was not a luxury available to the Chinese sage.

The same immersion in the daily affairs of society as subaltern officials which tends to exclude speculative thinking also can obstruct the development of rational methodology. F. S. C. Northrop draws a distinction between intuitional and postulational reasoning to account for the difference of methodological consciousness between China and the West. Postulational reasoning establishes the validity of a chain of reasoned ideas by reducing some to primitive concepts (taken as postulates) and developing their implication in chains of deductions. Intuitional thinking, on the other hand, arrives at its certainties, not by deductive analysis, but by the apprehension of entire situations in acts of immediate apprehension.[14] So far as this distinction had validity, Chinese philosophy can be said to be of an intuitional type.

Since its task was ever to apply traditional wisdom to changing experience, Chinese philosophy expressed its insights in sayings or letters rather than in formal philosophic works.

The whole book of *Lao-tzu* consists of aphorisms, and most of the chapters of the *Chuang-Tzu* are full of allusions and illustrations. . . . Suggestiveness, not articulateness, is the ideal of all Chinese art, whether it be poetry, painting, or anything else.[15]

The sayings of Confucius's *Analects* and the cryptic aphorisms of *Lao-tze* are not conclusions drawn from premises. They are emblematic expressions to be taken entirely by themselves for their rich connotations. Under circumstances where the emblematic expression was valued more highly than the logically established conclusion, problems of methodology so inseparable from the philosophical thought of the West could not rise to the center of experience.

Under the influence of its philosophic impetus toward bold speculation on the one hand and methodological precision on the other, the Western mind was compelled to confront a series of unique problems.

The Problems of Western Philosophy

The conditions of its origin and development virtually insured that the nature of life and death, of the constitution of the world, of its destiny, in fact all the problems the human imagination could conjure up, would become the proper province of philosophy. Among the great problems that have dominated Western thought as a result are the nature of ultimate reality; the problems of speculative philosophy in its most comprehensive sense (metaphysics) and its most vigorous branch, the theory of being (ontology); the nature of knowledge (epistemology) and method; the nature and constitution of values.

Metaphysical and Ontological Issues

Metaphysics is generally traced to a work of Aristotle bearing the same title. Like his compatriots, Aristotle did not draw a sharp distinction between the examination of the ordinary objects of experience (the subject matter of physics) and the ultimate properties of reality taken in its most general sense. Aristotle thought the particular sciences treated the special aspects of reality, metaphysics or "first philosophy" studies, "being" in its most comprehensive sense.

To the Greek mind, the most significant distinction that could be drawn between the modes of being was that between changing being (the mode of being of the ordinary objects of experience and the subject matter of natural philosophy or physics) and the changeless being (the mode of being belonging to the highest form of reality). Closely allied to this distinction between changeless and changing beings was the classical distinction between "substance" (that which remains unchanged through various transformations of a thing and provides its permanent identity) and "accident" (those qualities of things which change).

Philosophers of the nineteenth and twentieth centuries have tended to reverse the order of priority assigned by the Greeks to the modes of being which valued the unchanging over the changing. Process and change are taken as fundamental, and the static aspects of things are taken to be only temporary conditions. Associated with this re-evaluation is the tendency in recent scientific theories to place emphasis on energy, dynamic processes, and evolution in their explanations of various categories of events.

Some speculative philosophers (the phenomenologists) draw a distinction between *essence* (what a thing is) and *existence* (whether it is). These are assigned a very different status from that of the classical notions of changeless and changing being, though they may seem somewhat similar. It is believed that *essences* are directly given in experience (sensual as well as conceptual) and that existence is established only in secondary reflection.

Finally, the Existentialists and various thinkers whom they conceive as their spiritual ancestors (such as Pascal) have placed emphasis on the contrast between immediate reality of personal consciousness (*Dasein* or "being there" in Heidegger's language) and the world of facts and events that is experienced not directly but inferred. This clearly has close affinities with the phenomenological distinction between *essence* and *existence.*

However, while some contemporary philosophers have continued the task of seeking to characterize the modes of being in an ultimate sense, others have broken sharply with this metaphysical tradition. Since the days of Hume and Kant, at the close of the eighteenth century, positions critical to all metaphysical positions have repeatedly been advanced. Metaphysics, in fact, is often defined as the study of events which cannot be shown to exist (the logical positivists) or of nonnatural objects (G. E. Moore). The logical positivists have, perhaps, been most extreme in their scepticism of traditional metaphysics. Some have maintained that all metaphysical statements are purely verbal in character without any reference beyond the words themselves. Their opponents have, at times, insisted that the anti-metaphysicians have carried their scepticism to metaphysical lengths.

Epistemological and Methodological Issues

The conditions which favored the rise of classical philosophy sent it on a course toward heightened epistemological and methodological consciousness. The classical philosophers applied to their thought the Greek demand to see things whole in terms of rational and formal principles. They were convinced that the thought process itself supplies the grounds for truth. Almost from the beginning they isolated the problem of universals, the nature of general concepts, and their relation to particulars or concrete events.

Plato was well aware of the fact that general names such as "man," "horse," and "tree" do not designate objects which can be observed. One observes particular objects with all their special qualities of size, shape, color, and changeability. Plato took the position that general terms designate objects of a higher reality than ordinary objects. Individual objects are inferior copies of these ideal objects.

Aristotle objected to this separation of ideal and actual realms, arguing that the referents of general names do exist in concrete reality, though they are never experienced as such. General names refer to universal properties of specific things, objective features of nature. Terms such as "man," "horse," "tree," and the like designate an analytically separable property of actual realities.

In the medieval universities accompanying the attempt to synthesize Christian theology with the transmitted literatures of antiquity, the problem of universals was taken up once more. The *realists* advanced a position bearing many similarities with that of Aristotle, that general terms designate actual entities existing in nature. The *nominalists,* on the other hand, made a serious break not only with the realists but with the classical positions, urging that universals do not designate anything in nature; they are only names. Unlike Plato, however, they did not assign ideal objects to a higher level of reality. A third group of medieval thinkers took the position that universals are neither words nor things, but signs of concepts, of thoughts in the mind. However, these concepts refer to actual situations outside the mind. Advocates of the position called themselves *conceptualists.*

Many of the empiricist philosophers of the contemporary world take a position close to the nominalistic or conceptualistic position and extend their reflection along lines quite in accord with Ockham's view that nothing exists in nature outside the mind other than individual things. General terms have reference to entities that are logical or linguistic in nature.[16]

The attempt to establish the nature of general concepts was inseparable from the Greek ideal of bringing the entire world of thought into formal, rational synthesis. Both the Platonic view that universals exist prior to concerted reality and Aristotle's that they exist in reality were consistent with the endeavor of Aristotle's *Posterior Analytics.* He undertook to demonstrate the harmonious synthesis of all human knowledge on the basis of self-evident principles. Aristotle assumed that the axiomatic methods applied equally to objects of experience and to conceptual objects—a view consistent with his notion that general objects exist "in things," or Plato's that they exist prior to things.

However, the rise of the modern temper was inseparable from the discovery that the problems of the empirical world cannot be solved by deduction from self-evident principles. This same discovery was a component in reopening the problem of universals and the differentiation of the *nominalistic* and *conceptualistic* position from the *realistic* (the close counterpart of both Platonic and Aristotelian positions). The artisans and artists who moved to the center stage in the drama of contemporary man in his dawn period and the scientist who eventually took their place relied on systematic experimentalism (rather than deductive reasoning from first principles) for solution of their empirical problems.

Contemporary philosophy is frequently traced from Descartes, who sought to carry out the ancient project of demonstrating the harmonious totality of knowledge in a manner which fused the classic and modern temper. The four principles laid down by Descartes in his *Discourse on Method* were intended to achieve this objective.

> Instead of the great number of precepts of which Logic is composed, I believed that I should find the four which I shall state quite sufficient, provided that I adhered to a firm and constant resolve never on any single occasion to fail in their observance. The first of these was to accept nothing as true which I did not clearly recognize to be so. . . . The second was to divide up each of the difficulties which I examined into as many parts as possible . . . that it might be resolved in the best manner possible. The third was to carry on my reflections in due order, commencing with objects that were the most simple and easy to understand, in order to rise little by little, or by degrees, to knowledge of the most complex. . . . The last was in all cases to make enumerations so complete and reviews so general that I should be certain of having omitted nothing.[17]

Descartes' program was intended to embrace the ordinary world of physical objects as well as the world of concepts in a single comprehensive system of explanation.

The great drama of contemporary philosophy unfolded in a succession of varieties which attended attempts to carry out Descartes's program. Karl Jaspers has observed: "This identification of modern science and modern philosophy with their old aspiration to total knowledge was catastrophic for both of them."[18] In modern philosophy an early rift appeared between the rationalists and the empiricists as various thinkers sought to attack the problem from the standpoint of conceptual or empirical perspectives respectively. Members of these schools quickly found it necessary to set aside one or the other of the major categories of objects, depending on their starting points.

Nevertheless, the attempts to synthesize the world of thought from rationalistic and empiricist perspectives had significant methodological consequences. The rationalists played an important role in the extension of logical and mathematical modes of analysis as the drive toward rational integration sought to a break down the walls between various areas of thought, spurring the search for a universal language and an integration of logical and mathematical modes of thought into a single system. The empiricists played a significant part in the attempt to extend scientific methodology into an all-embracing empirical method. They were, also, quick to apply developments in probability theory to empirical analysis.

Meanwhile, the special sciences quietly set aside the total study of natural objects for systematic empirical programs of study of limited scope, moving step by step in the solution of their problems. At times this humble step by step process brought them into conflict with the general drift of contemporary philosophy.

The Problem of Values

The comprehensive program of the Western philosopher which led him to include all knowledge in his scope made ethics, the study of those properties which characterize action as "right" and the ends of action as "good," into a basic province of his endeavor.

Aristotle's ethical rationalism which brought classical theory into synthesis was quite accorded with the general Greek demand for wholeness, rationality, and formal symmetry. Man's good, that which is desired for itself, Aristotle reasoned, is happiness. Moreover, the behavior which yields enduring happiness is in accord with virtue. The highest virtues are intellectual and moral. Wisdom is the highest intellectual virtue. The highest good for man is the balanced development of his potentialities, which means the exercise of his capacities under the guidance of his reason. Aristotle was by no means inclined to visualize man's virtue as the development of his intellectual prowess at the expense of his other capacities. The development of the whole man, of all of his capacities under the control of his reason was, he believed, possible to man only under the condition of society.

Another doctrine development in the classical world by the Cyreniacs and Epicureans, hedonism, identified the good with the pleasant. This doctrine, like Aristotle's eudaemonism (the notion that happiness is the product of an active life under the guidance of reason), was by no means conceived as the pursuit of sensual pleasure but identified with the satisfaction yielded by a balanced reason-guided life. Epicurus, for example, held that the pleasures of the contemplative, philosophic mind, while less intense than the carnal delights, were superior in long-range satisfaction. Once again the Greek emphasis on the rational, responsible life was evident. In the modern world the utilitarians developed doctrines which were somewhat similar to classical hedonism.

Classical ethical theories rest on the division between the ideal and concrete worlds. The good was assigned to the world of the spirit; the happiness produced by the exercise of the bodily functions or the pleasures they afforded belonged among the lower forms of good. The Good, the True, the Beautiful, in their pure forms, belonged to the world of the spirit.

In the modern world the elevation of the world of practical action to a status of equality to the world of the mind called the classical hierarchization of values into question. Modern ethical theories with considerable frequency seek to derive the good from nature (ethical naturalism) in direct contrast to the classical attempt to derive the good from the ideal (ethical rationalism or idealism). In accord with the new emphasis on behavior, many modern ethical theorists have endeavored to establish the nature of ethical forms in terms of the quality of action (pleasantness), the consequences of action (utilitarianism and instrumentalism) or in terms of the underlying motives that led to it. The ethics of Immanuel Kant were of the last type: the properties of motive of intent provided the central clue to the right.

To Kant only acts which proceed from a sense of duty qualify as moral acts. In search of a general principle which will indentify an act as good, Kant called into question happiness (a consequence of action) or pleasure (a qualitative accompaniment of behavior). Only acts performed out of a sense of duty and in terms of the principle that one would be willing to see it become a universal law are right. In the end only one thing is good, the good will itself. Hence, one can formulate the principle: so act that one treats another person only as an end, never as a means.

The attempt to integrate ethical knowledge into a single system along with other forms of knowledge was carried out from quite distinct positions in the ancient and modern world. The ancients sought to assimilate the good to the ideal realm of the spirit; the moderns to assimilate it to the world of nature. The failure of both of these enterprises has led to the frequent appearance of forms of ethical "intuitionism," the view that ethical propositions are directly recognized as valid without further proof. A contemporary form of ethical intuitionism was developed by G. E. Moore. Positivistic-inclined thinkers, on the other hand, in view of the failure to reduce ethical propositions to logical or empirical forms, have often inclined to assign them neither logical nor empirical standing, but to consider them to be mere expressions of feeling.

Philosophy and Science

Western metaphysics, epistemology, methodology, and ethics arose and assumed their peculiar forms in considerable measure because of the total conception of knowledge that dominated Western philosophy. The problems of value, of empirical fact, and of logical conceptualization could not be isolated from one another under such circumstances. In the confrontation of these various forms of conceptual activity, their distinctive properties were lifted to an intensified self-consciousness.

The inclination to treat thought as a unity was also critical to the rise of science. The classical temper and its axiomatic method fell short of science in a basic respect. Science deals with matters of fact that can only be settled on the basis of empirical investigation. However, factual investigation alone falls short of science. Science consists of investigation of a special type that draws its inspiration in part both from the classical and modern temper. As science took shape it developed the ideal of logically deriving its hypotheses from a minimum set of principles, submitting them, however, to systematic empirical testing.

In his essay on the relation between "Philosophy and Science," Jaspers argued that science brought into the world something not found Asia, in antiquity, nor in the Middle Ages.[19] Among the properties of science, in Jaspers's opinion, are: every fact is a potential object of study; by definition it is an unfinished progress toward the infinite; it strives to integrate its findings into a universal frame of reference; it attaches little value to mere possibilities, recognizing only definite and concrete knowledge after it has been proved on the basis of investigation; it is applicable to all phenomena; and it consists in the search for reliable knowledge on the basis of unprejudiced inquiry without preconceived ideas.

The application of science has established one area of research after another as a recognized area of endeavor equipped to develop under its own impetus with little or no relation to philosophy. Such masses of tested information have been established by the special sciences that philosophers can no longer presume to deal effectively with the contents of them all.

> Now that we know how science obtains its universal validity, it has become evident that philosophy cannot stand up against judgment by these criteria. It deals in empty ideas, because it sets up undemonstrable hypotheses, it disregards experience, it seduces by illusions, it takes possession of energies needed for genuine investigation and squanders them in empty talk about the whole.[20]

In the face of the development of the special sciences, philosophy has tended to withdraw to limited tasks. Of its traditional content, in the opinion of many, only the history of philosophy and the preservation of ancient works for aesthetic purposes remains. Some contemporary philosophers, Jaspers observes, pay tribute to scientific trends by rejecting traditional thought systems and seeking to give philosophy itself an exact foundation. Such scientifically inclined philosophers reserve for philosophy the disciplines of logic, epistemology, and at times, phenomenology, which seem to apply to all the sciences. Jaspers notes, "Today many thinkers regard symbolic logic as the whole of philosophy."[21]

Other philosophers have reacted to the rise of science by going to opposite extremes, seeking to save philosophy by dropping all claims by philosophy to scientific standing. In contrast to science, philosophy, they maintain, is based on feeling, intuition, imagination, and genius. It is conceptual magic, not knowledge. It is the *élan vital* (Bergson); it is "resolute acceptance of death" (Heidegger). Jaspers tried for himself to avoid both alternatives: the unresisting submission to science or its radical rejection. Either alternative, he thinks, spelled the death of philosophy. He proposed, rather, to take pure science as an unquestioned starting point for contemporary thought, but to add a pure philosophy to it.

> Philosophy is not only less but also more than science, namely, as the source of a truth that is inaccessible to scientifically binding knowledge.

It is this philosophy that is meant in such definitions as: To philosophize is to learn how to die or to rise to godhead—or to know being qua being. The meaning of such definitions is: Philosophical thought is inward action; it appeals to freedom; it is a summons to transcendence.[22]

Jasper's position on the relations between philosophy and science reflects his desire to retain both: philosophy as the consolation of the intelligent man before the ultimate problems of his existence, science as a discipline giving man unparalleled powers over the conditions of his material existence. Hence Jaspers could not accept "scientific philosophy " even though he wishes to accept various developments in symbolic logic, analytical philosophy, and the philosophy of science as significant additions to human knowledge. To reduce philosophy to "scientific philosphy" as conceived by many of its advocates would be to set aside some of philosophy's age-old problems. Jaspers's solution is to retain both as two spheres of the individual's mental life, but keeping them distinct and separate from one another. To bring them together into one perspective, he insists, was the tragedy of modern philosophy. "Descartes did not understand modern science," as it is illustrated by the investigations of Galileo. Descartes's "own work had in spirit little to do with modern science, although as a creative mathematician he helped to advance this science."[23] The confusion, Jaspers believes, was still manifest in the work of Kant who was caught in a "totalist conception of science."[24] Philosophy and science, Jaspers feels, must do their distinctive work despite one another.

Jaspers's solution to the problem of simultaneously saving both philosophy and science is to shift responsibility for both to the individual. Philosophy and science are urged to be intrinsically antagonistic. Yet the individual requires each to be a whole man. Hence, the individual is urged to internalize both as requirements of the different sizes of his nature somehow or other sealing off each from direct bearing on the other. What it means to demand of the individual that he be at once a mystic and a hard-headed empiricist is not examined.

In his discussion Jaspers repeats one of the laments of many contemporary philosophers, that perhaps the whole enterprise of Western philosophy since Descartes was vain and doomed from the beginning. However, this cannot be the whole story, for the romance of the Western mind rested in considerable measure on its total confrontation of the human condition. Many discoveries were made that would hardly have been forthcoming in any other way. Science itself, which transformed traditional philosophy into an anachronism, was in part a product of this confrontation. Finally, sociology, which may perhaps be the last great creation of traditional philosophy, was a product of its ancient aspiration for total knowledge.

The Birth of Sociology

It is conventional to treat sociology as beginning with the work of August Comte. This is somewhat arbitrary for every major movement of human thought has many anticipations. Nevertheless, Comte's grandiose synthesis of ideas captured the imagination of many nineteenth-century intellectuals. After Comte sociology continued to develop without a break.

All the basic elements of the Western philosophic spirit were present in Comte's formulations: the total conception of knowledge; the metaphysical inclinations; the positivistic bias. Comte's synthesis came at a period when deep-seated uneasiness was spreading about the aspiration to bring all these issues under a single roof. There seems little doubt that one source of the appeal of sociology, despite the many crudities in its early forms, was its aspiration for total knowledge at a time when this hope was fading.

In his Course in Positive Philosophy,[25] Comte proposed a program of bringing about a total synthesis of all the branches of science as the first step in bringing order out of social chaos. The sciences were to be arranged in a pyramid in terms of the comparative generality and complexity or abstractness and concreteness of the knowledge of each. The most general and abstract of all knowledge, knowledge which applies to all other disciplines, Comte maintained, was mathematics. Resting on a foundation of mathematics, a series of successively more complex disciplines arose through physics, chemistry, biology to psychology and sociology. Only persons thoroughly grounded in the total system of the sciences were ultimately able to approach society in the proper spirit. Conceptual, empirical, ethical, and aesthetic knowledge are conceived to form a single unified system. Comte assigned to sociology the task of both clarifying the unity of knowledge and bringing order to society. W. P. Montague quite correctly saw Comte's enterprise as essentially metaphysical. "It is this binding or unifying function," Montague maintained, "which metaphysics seeks to perform."[26]

While pursuing an uninhibited metaphysical analysis, Comte vigorously advocated a thoroughgoing positivistic program. He insisted that metaphysics had no place in science or in sociology which should confine its analyses purely to what is phenomenally present without recourse to hidden essences or principles. Comte identified the period of the French Revolution as a metaphysical stage in the development of human thought and society. A positive science of society was believed by Comte to be essential to the permanent elimination of such revolutionary upheavals.

At the same time that he tilted his lances against metaphysics, Comte conceived total society or humanity or mankind (including its past history as an entity) organic in character and forming a single unit. The critical law of the development of humanity was progress. Comte's humanity was a metaphysical entity; his law of progress an ideology. Not only were metaphsical and value problems, thus, retained in Comte's sociology, but various ancient epistemological and methodological issues were restored as unavoidable problems of social theory.

At the very time that the philosophic aspiration for total knowledge was being called into question, sociology, representing one of the great unitary systems of thought of the nineteenth century, was a direct product of its spirit. The origin of sociology is directly traceable to the spirit of philosophy. In the very act of its creation sociology was saddled with the distinct problems of Western thought. When the edifice of traditional philosophy collapsed under the revolutionary upheavals of science, a new edifice, sociology, was erected on its ruins to house all the ancient problems which continue to plague the modern mind.

Notes

1. For details see "The Indian Guru" in Don Martindale, *Social Life and Cultural Change* (Princeton, N. J.: D. Van Nostrand, 1962), pp. 163–238.

2. Digha Nikaya of the Pali Canon, no. i, pp. 53–54. Quoted by A. L. Basham, *The Wonder That Was India* (New York: Grove Press, 1959), p. 296.

3. Fung Yu-lan, *A Short History of Chinese Philosophy* (New York: Macmillan, 1948), p. 2.

4. Ibid., p. 3.

5. Ibid.

6. Ibid., p. 4.

7. For further details see "The Chinese Mandarin," in Martindale, *Social Life and Cultural Change*, pp. 93–162.

8. Fung Yu-lan, *History of Chinese Philosophy*, p. 19.

9. Ibid., p. 20.

10. Ibid., p. 21.

11. Max Weber, *The City*, trans. Don Martindale and Gertrud Neuwirth (Glencoe, Ill.: The Free Press, 1958), p. 229.

12. Fung Yu-lan, *History of Chinese Philosophy*, p. 7. The question from Confucius is from James Legge, trans., *The Chinese Classics*, vol. 1, *Confucian Analects* (Oxford: The Clarendon Press, 1893). The quotation from Mencius is from James Legge, trans., *The Chinese Classics* (Oxford: The Clarendon Press, 1895), vol. 2.

13. Quoted by Fung Yu-lan, ibid., p. 10.

14. F. S. C. Northrop, "The Complementary Emphases of Eastern Intuitional Philosophy and Western Scientific Philosophy," *Philosophy, East and West*, ed. C. A. Moore (Princeton, N.J.: Princeton University Press, 1946), p. 187.

15. Fung Yu-lan, *History of Chinese Philosophy*, p. 12.

16. M. H. Carre, *Nominalists and Realists* (London: Oxford University Press, 1946), p. 106.

17. Ralph M. Eaton, ed., *Descartes Selections* (New York: Scribner's, 1927), pp. 16–17.

18. Karl Jaspers, *Way to Wisdom*, trans. Ralph Mannheim (New Haven: Yale University Press, 1954), p. 153.

19. Ibid., pp. 151 ff.

20. Ibid., pp. 147–48.

21. Ibid., p. 149.

22. Ibid., p. 162.

23. Ibid., p. 153.

24. Ibid.

25. August Comte, *The Positive Philosophy of August Comte*, trans. Harriet Martineau (London: J. Chapman, 1853).

26. W. P. Montague, *The Ways of Things* (Englewood Cliffs, N. J.: Prentice-Hall, 1940), pp. 10–11.

Selected Bibliography

Aristotle. *The Collected Works of Aristotle.* Oxford: The Clarendon Press, 1908–1931.

Ayer, A. J. *Language, Truth, and Logic.* London: Victor Gollancz, 1948.

Basham, A. L. *The Wonder That Was India.* New York: Grove Press, 1959.

Bergson, Henri. *An Introduction to Metaphysics.* Translated by T. E. Hulme. New York: G. P. Putnam's Sons, 1912).

Comte, August. *The Positive Philosophy of August Comte.* Translated by Harriet Martineau. London: J. Chapman, 1853.

Jaspers, Karl. *The Way to Wisdom.* Translated by Ralph Mannheim. New Haven: Yale University Press, 1954.

Martindale, Don. *Social Life and Cultural Change.* Princeton, N. J.: D. Van Nostrand, 1962.

Weber, Max. *The City.* Translated by Don Martindale and Gertrud Neuwirth. Glencoe: The Free Press, 1958.

Yu-lan, Fung. *A Short History of Chinese Philosophy.* New York: Macmillan, 1948.

2

Max Weber:
Sociology's Last Puritan

"Max Weber," says Daniel Rossides, "is the only non-metaphysical social scientist of modern times (except Montesquieu), the only one to develop a genuinely scientific social science."[1] Although some students also have described Weber as the greatest sociologist of all time, there is no great virtue in such evaluations. Few things are more bootless than invidious distinctions in the field of science, for when a scientist of the past is turned into an apotheosized superman he is transformed into the center of a cult. The effect is at once to devalue the works of other thinkers and to transform those of the cult center into sources of dogma. Max Weber was an outstanding member of the generation that transformed sociology into a professional discipline. His work remains a part of the living heritage of sociology, still serving as a source of much vital theorizing and research. His works should not be sanctified and placed beyond use.

A Chronological Review of
Max Weber's Life and Death

Max Weber was born into a middle-class family in Erfurt, Thuringia, April 21, 1864. The family on his father's side had been linen mer-

27

chants and textile manufacturers. Members of his mother's family had been teachers, theologians, and small officials. Weber's father trained as a jurist, became an effective politician, serving in the municipal diet of Berlin, in the Prussian diet, and finally in the Reichstag. Max Weber was reared in the cosmopolitan atmosphere created by the many important political and academic persons who frequented the parental household and broadened by the extensive travels of the family.

After finishing the Gymnasium at Berlin-Charlottenburg in 1882, Max Weber's university studies were pursued at Heidelberg. There he joined a duelling fraternity, participating in patterns of status imitation of the Junker aristocracy which typified upper-class German university students. His undergraduate university studies were continued at Strassburg, where he served his year in the army and received his officer's commission, and then completed the requirements at Berlin and Goettingen. His studies concentrated on law, economics, and history. In 1886 Max Weber began postgraduate studies of law at the University of Berlin, completing his Ph.D. dissertation on *The History of Trading Companies during the Middle Ages* in 1889. He passed his second examination in law in 1890 and began teaching at the University of Berlin. His habilitation thesis was on *The History of Roman Agrarian Institutions* (1891). During the same period (1891–1892), he conducted an investigation of the conditions of agrarian workers in the East Elbe area for the *Verein für Sozialpolitik*, a private reform group.

The early 1890s were a period of intensive work for Max Weber. In addition to his teaching he practiced law in Berlin and served as legal consultant in an official investigation of the stock market. Several essays on the stock market were a product of this experience.[2] He continued his researches on the agricultural workers of Eastern Germany, he participated in the Evangelical-Social Conferences on social policy, and he was active in the Christian Social Party. He was married to Marianne Schnitger, and in 1893 he became Professor of Commercial and German Law at the University of Berlin. He moved the next year, becoming Professor of Political Economics at Freiburg University (1894). In 1897 he was called as Professor of Political Science at Heidelberg University as successor to Karl Knies.

In 1897, shortly after the death of his father, Weber fell ill with a nervous disorder. For the rest of his life Weber tended to alternate between periods of nervous collapse, travel, and intense work. His state of psychic exhaustion was such that in 1898 and 1899 the university granted him leave with pay. The Webers traveled to Venice, and he returned apparently improved, but when he took up his duties he soon collapsed again more severely than before. For a short period in 1899 he entered a mental institution. The following summer he traveled in Italy and Switzerland. He felt so improved that in 1902 he was prepared to take up his teaching duties at Heidelberg once again. However, there were further setbacks, leading him to resign his professorship. He was made an honorary professor at Heidelberg in 1903.

In 1904 Weber was asked to join with Werner Sombart and Edgar Jaffe in editorship of the *Archiv für Sozialwissenschaft und Sozialpolitik*, which had been failing. Primarily under Weber's direction, it was transformed into the foremost social science journal in Germany, comparable to *L'Aneé Sociologique* in France and *The American Journal of Sociology* in the United States. In 1904 Weber visited the United States and addressed the St. Louis Congress of Arts and Science on "The Relations of the Rural Community to Other Branches of Social Science." The same year Weber undertook intense researches and writing in connection with his editorship. He completed a major essay on methods and the problem of objectivity in the social sciences and the first half of his most famous essay, *The Protestant Ethic and the Spirit of Capitalism*.

Stimulated by the Russian Revolution the following year, Weber quickly learned Russian and produced for the *Archiv* two major essays on Russia: "The Situation of the Bourgeois Democracy in Russia" and "Russia's Transition to Sham Constitutionalism." He completed major essays on religious groupings in 1906. An analysis of historical materialism and social science methodology was carried through in 1907. An essay on "Agrarian Conditions in Antiquity" was written for the *Handwörterbuch der Staatswissenschaften* (3d ed., vol. 1, 1909) in 1908. Also in 1908 Weber made a survey on "The Adjustment and Selection of Workers in Large-Scale Industrial Establishments" for the Society for Social Policy. He undertook a major investigation of industrial psychology in his grandfather's linen factory in Westphalia.

In 1908 Weber also took an active part in the deliberations leading to the establishment of the German Sociological Society. He assumed responsibility (1909) for organizing and editing (for Paul Siebeck) a series of studies on the Foundations of Social Economics. His own contribution to the series, *Wirtschaft und Gesellschaft*, was published posthumously. In 1910 he played a leading role in setting the tone of the discussion and directing the research orientations of the first meeting of the German Sociological Society.

In 1911 Weber began his extensive studies of the influence of the world religions on economic ethics. These were eventually collected and published posthumously in the three volumes of *Gesamelte Auf-sätze zur Religionssoziologie*. Also, between 1911 and 1913, he worked ahead on his contribution to *Foundations of Social Econom-ics (Grundriss der Sozialökonomik)*. His *Sociology of Law, System-atic Sociology of Religion, Sociology of Economics, The Sociology of Music*, and the methodological discussions of *Categories of Inter-pretative Sociology* were all composed in this connection.

In 1914 Max Weber participated in the discussion of values spon-sored by The Vienna Society for Social Policy. With the outbreak of war, as an over-age reserve officer, he was commissioned and placed as officer in charge of nine hospitals in the Heidelberg area. The bureaucratic structure he created was dissolved in a reorganization in 1915, and Weber was retired from active duty. He returned to his studies of the world religions and published in the *Archiv* (1916–1917) essays on Confucianism, Hinduism, and Buddhism.

In 1917 Max Weber accepted a visiting professorship at the Uni-versity of Vienna for the summer session, returning to teaching for the first time since his breakdown. He lectured on "Positive Criticism of the Materialistic Interpretation of History" and "The Sociology of the State." He was developing into a national figure and was invited to participate in deliberations of the Ministry of Interior in Berlin. In 1918 and 1919 he lectured in behalf of the German Democratic Party and worked on essays on *Ancient Judaism*. In 1919, to the students' organization of the University of Munich, he delivered addresses on "Science as a Vocation" and "Politics as a Vocation." He was a member of the German Peace Delegation to Versailles. He also was appointed to the University of Munich as successor to Lujo Bren-tano. His lectures on economic history were worked up at the re-quest of students and were published as *A General Economic History*.

A number of family crises and responsibilities accumulated for the Webers in 1919. Weber's mother died in the fall of 1919. Shortly after, his sister (whose husband had recently died in battle) also died. The Webers decided to adopt the four orphaned children of his sister, only to be plagued by later doubts which led to the delay of the reception of the children into the household. In June, 1920, Weber caught cold, and by the time it was diagnosed as deep-seated pneumonia, it was too late to hope for his recovery. He died June 14, 1920. H. Stuart Hughes raises some interesting questions about the events surrounding Weber's death:

> Weber proved a cheerful patient; he did not fight the illness. In mid-June, 1920, he lay dead. . . . Weber's sudden death is conventionally

described as a career cut short at its very height. In terms of professional accomplishment, this is undoubtedly true. . . . But in personal terms, the matter is more perplexing. Did Weber have a sense that his new responsibilities were threatening to overwhelm him? Was he in his last months living in dread of a relapse into his earlier malady, to which anything, even death, would be preferable? Did he unconsciously long for release from his sudden eminence? At this very moment, Freud was publishing his speculations on the "death instinct" in human beings. We can only wonder.[3]

It adds very little to one's understanding of Max Weber or of his intellectual influence to decide that he spent his life under the torments of an Oedipus complex and died from a "death instinct." Moreover, it is somewhat risky, because Weber's psychological attitude during his last illness was one of "cheerful" resignation, to take this attitude as self-evidence of the presence of a death instinct. It is characteristic that pneumonia and other serious lung ailments are often accompanied by psychological attitudes of passive resignation.

The Genesis of
Max Weber's Energies and Point of View

There is some evidence from the biography of Max Weber by his wife, Marianne, from Weber's letters, and from the accounts of personal friends and associates that the intensity of his intellectual life rested in part in the degree to which personal problems coincided with the underlying social predicament of the stratum to which he belonged. When this occurs, an individual's subjective problems are objectified in his theories and his theories are fired with personal passion.

There were some anomalies in the German middle classes to which Max Weber belonged which may be elucidated by comparison with the fate of the middle classes in some other West European nations. The middle classes were the critical strata in the rise of contemporary national society. In France, in England, and in the United States they carried out the political revolutions which delivered the state into their hands, initiating the movement toward mass democracy. Though the German middle classes were among the first to develop in Europe, they were late in receiving political and social recognition in any way equivalent to that enjoyed elsewhere.

The German city and her middle-class strata developed early, for the Italian wave of city development was soon followed by parallel movements in German hands. At the same time, in the feudalized Holy Roman Empire, Germany had inherited from the Middle Ages a political structure which blocked the developments of nationalism of a contemporary type and the access of the middle class to positions of political opportunity and responsibility. Germany lagged behind her Western neighbors (France and England) in the formation of a nation of contemporary type, despite the rise of cultural nationalism (in the face of frustrated political aspirations) by its middle-class strata. When the German state took shape in the early nineteenth century, moreover, it was taken over into the hands of the landed aristocrats. Middle-class, urban strata were granted only a minor voice in the destiny of the nation.

In 1830 and again in 1848 the German middle classes made their bid for equal recognition in the German state. When their aspirations were frustrated and members of the class were subject to persecution, many individuals of the German middle classes migrated to North America, bringing with them valuable professions and skills. Marx, who had begun his career as a spokesman for radical elements of the German middle classes, was embittered by the consequences of the 1848 experience. He thereafter gave up the notion that it was possible to work within the framework of the state.

Thus, while the middle classes in France, England, and, above all, the United States had moved into the center of national and economic affairs, the German middle classes found themselves blocked. In part, they compensated for the frustrations in their political and economic situation by exaggerated cultural achievement. At the same time, successful members of the upper middle class often imitated the uncultivated, agrarian crudeness all too characteristic of the Junker aristocracy. This was particularly evident in circles of upper-middle-class university students, who joined duelling fraternities and spent much time beer drinking, gambling, getting into debt, and otherwise imitating modes of deportment identified with the rural nobility.

The effect of these developments in Germany was to establish a peculiar division in the mental set of the middle classes: polarizing them in terms of attitudes of expedient crudeness and exaggerated rank consciousness in social and political affairs, and of a principled sensitivity and religious intensity in cultural concerns.

Weber belonged to the German middle class. His worldly, secular-minded lawyer father, active in civic and national politics, oriented toward the public concerns and affairs, pragmatically ready to compromise principle whenever it was expedient, expressed one phase of orientations of this middle class. His sensitive, shy, pious mother oriented toward letters, cultural concerns, and things of the spirit, forever locating problems of principle above the expediencies of everyday affairs, epitomized the other pole in the middle-class German mentality. The conflict and estrangement which developed between Max Weber's parents was a source of keen discomfort to him. It may, perhaps, be significant that Weber's illness became acute shortly after his father's death. Prior to his father's death, a sharp altercation had taken place between father and son over the father's treatment of Weber's mother. Weber was seized with severe guilt feelings over the affair. Whatever the influence may be, two major dimensions of the middle-class mind—expediency in sociopolitical concerns and principled sensitivity in spiritual matters—were dramatized in Weber's parents.

While Germany was divided into Protestant and Roman Catholic, as was the rest of Western Europe, a number of factors cooperated to give religion a somewhat greater intensity in Germany than was usual elsewhere in Western Europe. Many observers have noted the tendency for Germans to go to extremes in religious matters; toward dogmatic atheism or religious fanaticism without convenient stopping points between.

Italy, France, and Spain were predominantly Roman Catholic; England and the United States were predominantly Protestant. Religion is not usually a major issue in a community that is religiously homogeneous. Germany, however, was fairly close to a balance, being around 55 percent Protestant to 45 percent Roman Catholic. Under such circumstances the possibility always remains of the community being split approximately in half over religion.

Again, during the nineteenth century Protestantism was not only made into Germany's official religion, but Bismarck entered upon the dangerous experiment of attempting to stamp out Roman Catholicism. Bismarck's use of Protestantism as an instrument of political control placed underprivileged groups (such as laborers) in the position where they were not only economically and politically deprived, but where an antireligious construction was placed on attempts at self-improvement. One consequence of such policies was to drive many laborers into opposition to all religion, leading them to embrace atheistic philosophies. Karl Marx accurately summarized the German laborer's experience when he described religion as "the opiate of the masses."

On the other hand, the same official policies that drove many German workers to atheism served to turn many genuinely religious people away from official forms of religiosity—which were cynically used for political ends—toward a more purely personal religiosity.

Meanwhile, the cultural struggle between the Protestant and Roman Catholic branches of the community left a lingering concern as to the importance of religion.

The patterns of personal deportment in Germany were strongly determined after the sixteenth century by Protestantism with its point of gravity in the middle classes. Traditional Christianity promised religious salvation through observance of the sacraments and the mediation of the priesthood. The sacraments provided a religious framework for adjusting to the major life crises such as birth, marriage, and death. The priesthood was not only essential for their proper performance but stood by with the confessional to release emotional pressures. However, the perfection of the Christian life was open only to those who took a further step and turned away from the world to practice withdrawn asceticism for the glory of God and salvation of the soul. Protestantism changed all this, reducing the priesthood to a mere facilitating device not absolutely essential to salvation. It promoted the nonsacramental theory of salvation, making salvation ultimately an individual responsibility in all life spheres. Finally, it eliminated the concept of withdrawn asceticism practiced by a few as the perfection of the Christian life. It substituted the inner-worldly asceticism of all. The effect of these changes was to introduce a new religious intensity and significance to everyday conduct while responsibility was individualized.

Max Weber belonged to a generation whose members were still often reared in an atmosphere which transformed the Protestant ethos into second nature even while they were religiously emancipated.

Weber exemplified in relatively pure form the Protestant ethos when he plunged into work with something approximating a religious frenzy and spoke of "the need to feel crushed under the load of work."[4] Moreover, he reacted against the doctrines of Freud which he perceived as a disguised rehabilitation of the confessional with the scientist in the role of priest and the substitution of an ideal of "normality" or "health" for ethical responsibilities.[5] Implicit in this reaction to Freudian psychotherapy as a form of moral shoddiness is the ideal of the man of conscience.

It is not altogether clear what played the most important role in the build-up of tensions that drove Max Weber into semi-invalidism for so much of his life. Possibly the conflict between his parents had laid a foundation on which others could be arranged. His own emotional history also undoubtedly was accompanied by tension build-up. For some six years before his marriage to Marianne Schnitger, Max Weber was in love with a Strassburg cousin who had spent time in a mental hospital and who was recovering when he broke up with her. His relations with Marianne, a grand niece of Max Weber, Sr., were complicated by the fact that a friend had courted her and Max Weber found it painful to cut in. The fact that the women with whom he was emotionally involved belonged to the two branches of the family may well have served to pyramid the tensions. Persons raised on the Protestant ethic who have learned to turn the problems of their lives into purely private testing grounds of their sense of worth often lash themselves unmercifully for real or presumed shortcomings. In any case, Weber plunged into work for all the world as if in expiation for guilt and nourished a sense of inadequacy from the Sisyphean tasks he undertook. As a young scholar in Berlin, he imposed a burden of work on himself that no man could sustain for long: in addition to nineteen hours a week of teaching, he was participating in state examinations for lawyers and undertaking consultant work for government agencies and special research for private reform groups.

Weber was unusually equipped by circumstances and training to carry on his lone struggle toward self-clarification in terms of the most vital problems of his generation. The parental household was a center of intellectual and political ferment—among visitors to the household were Wilhelm Dilthey, Theodor Mommsen, H. Treitschke, Julian Schmidt, H. Sybel, and Friedrich Kapp. From the mother's branch of the family, the Strassburg branch, Weber was acquainted with theological literatures, problems, and disputes. He received his training in German universities at a time when the humanistic and historical traditions had been brought to a high level of perfection. His own degree was taken in law, where the whole historical movement had begun, but he was almost as well qualified in history, philosophy, and economics. Finally, Weber moved all his life at the center of active intellectual and artistic circles of pre-war Germany. At Berlin he was acquainted with Theodor Mommsen. While teaching at Freiburg University he came to know Hugo Münsterberg, Pastor Naumann, and Wilhelm Rickert. At Heidelberg his circle of friends included Georg Jellinek, Paul Hensel, Karl Neumann, Wilhelm Windelband, and Ernst Troeltsch. Among the visitors to the Webers were Robert Michels, Werner Sombart, Paul Hensel, Hugo Münsterberg, Karl Vossler, Georg Simmel, Paul Honigsheim, Karl Lowenstein, Georg Lukacs, Mina Tobler, Karl Jaspers, and others. Artists, philosophers, historians, psychiatrists, musicians, and many types of social scientists were drawn to the Weber sphere.

While a surprisingly large number of the most distinguished scholars and intellectuals of his generation were drawn to Weber and while they were universally impressed with the power of his mind and personality, as Julien Freund has observed: "There is no Weberian school, as there is a Marxist, a Comtian and even a Durkheimian school."[6] This remained true in the post-war period despite the ironic fact that "Many German university teachers vaunt the illustrious title of being a former student of Max Weber."[7]

Unquestionably the failure of Max Weber to found a school was in part related to the erratic course of his teaching career. After a relatively short period Weber stopped teaching in 1903 and did not resume teaching until a few months before his death in 1920. The institutionally located professor, particularly if engaged in training Ph.D. candidates, tends to be pressed in the direction of school formation. His efficiency is enhanced if he codifies his concepts and procedures into a dogma. Even if the master does not undertake this codification, his assistants and disciples may find it useful. When his former students move out into positions of their own, the school spreads in a sort of colonization process. Hence had Max Weber spent his career primarily as an institutional rather than a private scholar it is quite possible that the pressures for school formation, if not by him, but others associated with him, might have been irresistible. After Weber's death, under Karl Mannheim at Heidelberg this process was in fact underway until interrupted by the Nazis.

However, it is quite possible that the same factors in Max Weber's personality that made teaching so difficult produced an intellectual life that resisted codification. Weber, though denying personal religiosity, never lost the Protestant, and to some extent, monkish inclination to shift the arena of decisions on all issues to his inner conscience. This was a practice that had led many of the early Protestants to stand alone, naked before their consciences and their God, against the forces of this world in defiance of princes and kings. Weber seems never to have been able to yield the power of decision and responsibility to any institution's official ideological requirements. Hence, he repeatedly found himself standing alone. Freund observes:

Indeed, on a number of occasions Weber found himself completely isolated, abandoned by those who had called themselves his best friends. This isolation was no doubt due to his political attitude and, more particularly, to his hostility to the rash undertakings of Kaiser Wilhelm II. But he was similarly isolated even on the purely scientific terrain of the discussion of the concept of ethical neutrality, for instance at certain memorable meetings of the Association for Social Policy. Some of his positions on public affairs aroused the fury of nationalist students, who went so far as to invade his class-room to prevent him from lecturing.

A perusal of the pious biography written by his wife, Marianne Weber, affords but the merest inkling of the outbursts, revolts and scandals he provoked.[8]

Since Max Weber never lost the Puritan's tempermental conservativism, he was reluctant to abandon any position so long as it retained any value or any idea that retained a claim to truth. It was this conservatism rather than independence per se or exasperating ambivalence that led Weber to entertain simultaneously so many ideas and propositions that other thinkers found to be self-contradictory.

In all things and all circumstances, he was essentially independent, and this explains in part some of his apparently contradictory statements and attitudes. The same impulse prompted him to advocate both the shooting of the first Polish official to set foot in Danzig and the execution of Count von Arco, the assassin of Kurt Eisner, who had headed the revolutionary government of Bavaria. Again, although he detested Ludendorff, Weber was prepared to defend him against unjust attack. He actively opposed the exclusion of anarchists, socialists and Jews from university faculties, and had only contempt for the revolutionary movement that sprang up following the defeat of 1918. And while he came out in support of pacifist students, he advocated "chauvinism" should the peace be merely unilaterally imposed by the Allies.[9]

The temperamental inability to gloss over real or apparent contradictions seems to have been a component in turning teaching into a nightmare. When he accepted a full professorship at Freiburg University, Gerth and Mills observed: "He had an enormous load, working until very late. When Marianne urged him to get some rest, he would call out: 'If I don't work until one o'clock I can't be a professor.' "[10] Later, in 1896, when Weber accepted a chair at Heidelberg he pressed himself to even greater labors and over the summer fell ill with a psychic malady. Gerth and Mills observed: "He seemed to get better when the academic year began, but toward the end of the fall semester he collapsed from tension and remorse, exhaustion and anxiety. For his essentially psychiatric condition, doctors prescribed cold water, travel, and exercise. Yet Weber continued to experience the sleeplessness of an inner tension. For the rest of his life he suffered intermittently from severe depressions, punctuated by manic spurts of extraordinarily intense intellectual work and travel."[11] No man could hope to handle for long the task Weber imposed upon himself, to bring every real or apparent contradiction in the material he was supposed to teach into confrontation in his own mind in the attempt to resolve them.

If one were to characterize the style of the man, Weber's would seem most similar to the musical styles of the series of German composers from Bach to Beethoven. What began with the voice against voice counterpoint of Bach came to a climactic fulfillment in the polyphonic confrontations brought into the passionate synthesis of Beethoven. It was Weber's tendency to bring every apparent contradiction of theme or position or concept into confrontation and to unfold its tension as he searched for a point of unity satisfying to himself. It is little wonder that those who knew him were impressed by his external ferment but inner calm. In Freund's words: "Those who knew him say that he was like a volcano in constant eruption, at the same time retaining an inward calm which added to the confusion of those who argued with him."[12] One is inclined to observe that perhaps the image of a hurricane or typhoon with unusual violence in its outer winds and dead calm at the eye of the storm would be more appropriate.

At few times has Weber come closer to the characterization of his own style than in his perceptive essay on "Politics as a Vocation." Many of the most brilliant formulations of the essay occur in the course of the counterpointlike unfolding against one another of two contrasting styles of politics: a politics resting on an ethic of ultimate ends and a politics resting on an ethic of responsibility. A politics resting on an ethic of ultimate ends seeks only to do what is right; a politics resting on an ethic of responsibility withholds final judgment and seeks a maximum solution to the plural values in human situations. An ethic of ultimate ends often leads to tyranny; an ethic of responsibility often degenerates into pure expediency. A politics resting on an ethic of ultimate ends is a politics of the heart; one resting on an ethic of responsibility aiming at rational compromise is a politics of the head. While Weber in most ordinary cases observes, in a manner that would have won the approval of Immanuel Kant, that it is safer to follow the head rather than the heart, yet politics is not—and to this extent the proponents of a politics of ultimate ends are right—made by the head alone. Hence, so long as men continue their political activities, some will be found who maintain that they only undertake to do what is right, and if this has negative consequences it is unfortunate, but responsibility for these consequences does not fall upon them but upon those whom they serve and whose stupidity or baseness they are undertaking to eradicate. It is characteristic of the Weber style that having brought a confrontation of ideas to this point he makes the following observation. Referring to persons who advocate an ethic of ultimate ends, Weber observes:

I am under the impression that in nine out of ten cases I deal with windbags who do not fully realize what they take upon themselves but who intoxicate themselves with romantic sensations. From a human point of view this is not very interesting to me, nor does it move me profoundly. However, it is immensely moving when a *mature* man—no matter whether old or young in years—is aware of a responsibility for the consequences of his conduct and really feels such responsibility with heart and soul. He then acts by following an ethic of responsibility . . . and somewhere he reaches the point where he says: "Here I stand; I can do no other." That is something genuinely human and moving. And every one of us who is not spiritually dead must realize the possibility of finding himself at some time in that position. In so far as this is true, an ethic of ultimate ends and an ethic of responsibility are not absolute contrasts but rather supplements, which only in unison constitute a genuine man—a man who *can* have the "calling for politics."[13]

The pathos of this extraordinary passage derives from the fact that Weber was not simply formulating the ultimate requirements of a calling for politics, but, as he saw them, the ultimate requirements of the calling for science as well. It was the destiny of the man of science to stand alone with only his reason and his conscience, seeking to resolve the contradictions that swept in out of the world about him. As once the old Protestants had stood with their conscience and their God against the powers of this world, the man of science stood armed only with his puny wits against the irrationalities of the world. However, he was no longer sure that God stood at his side, for he was a Puritan in a nonreligious age.

The Main Drift of Recent Western Thought

The estimate of a thinker requires more than an examination of his biography. Ultimately he must be judged with respect to intellectual and social trends. It is necessary to chart briefly the main drift of Western thought to locate Max Weber's work.

The revolutions of the late eighteenth and nineteenth centuries were the turning point in contemporary developments. The prerevolutionary world was dominated by the politics of enlightened despotism. The state was, in principle, the private property of the kings. For their part, the kings were engaged in the creation of administrative and military structures which implemented their power and economic conditions (mercantilism, cameralism) which enhanced their financial independence. The middle classes which produced much of the liquid wealth that made the monarchies workable were largely without political power or social recognition. Under the enlightened despots a type of thinking became popular which is best described as rationalistic, individualistic, and reformist. Among the major objectives of enlightenment thought was the effort to remove the traditional obstacles to the reforms required by the new political and economic institutions.

The revolutions, which swept away some of the despots and threatened the position of others, brought the middle classes to political and social prominence. The new movements toward mass democracy and socialism were spawned by the revolutionary movements. Since the ideologies of revolution were framed out of the materials of rationalistic thought, rationalism went out of fashion once the revolution was over and the task of consolidating the new social order it had created was faced. A type of thinking best described as collectivistic appeared. It had two major forms: collectivistic and conservative (illustrated by Hegel and August Comte) and collectivistic and revolutionary (illustrated by Marx and Engels).

In the prerevolutionary period society was conceived to be a conscious association (contract) of similarly constituted rational individuals. In the postrevolutionary period (for both right- and left-wing groups) society was conceived to be a superindividual entity with properties not reducible to individuals. Individuals were increasingly viewed in the postrevolutionary world as irrational and emotional. Rationality was reconceptualized as an objective property of society. In the prerevolutionary period the basic method of thought was usually conceived as a process of analysis in terms of fundamental units. Hegel and Marx set much of the tone to methodological thought in the nineteenth century by arguing that the true method both of thought (and of reality) consisted of dialectical conflicts within the whole of the mind (or of social reality) which were overcome by more comprehensive syntheses.

In the late eighteenth and early nineteenth centuries in Germany, where the middle and intellectual classes were bearers of an insurgent cultural nationalism, such theoretical collectivism and a predisposition toward dialectical-synthetic methodology were characteristic. Hegel became the great spokesman for these strata. When an embittered individualist such as Schopenhauer attempted to criticize such collectivism, he was for some time simply thrust aside.

However, when their revolutionary bids for political and social recognition were largely frustrated after 1830 and 1848, the German middle classes became somewhat disillusioned with theoretical collectivism and dialectical methodologies. For the first time Schopen-hauer became popular. After the frustrations of 1870, the disillusionment deepened. In the late nineteenth century these dis-satisfactions increasingly took the form of a ferment in German thought represented by neo-idealistic and neo-Kantian trends.

In somewhat different ways both the neo-idealists and the neo-Kantians called into question the collectivistic assumptions of the early nineteenth century and offered alternatives to dialectical methodologies. The neo-idealists dropped the notion that the social and intellectual world forms a single great process in which thought moves by a synthesis of opposites. Rather, they argued there is no critical difference in the thought processes which deal with the mind and with nature. Nature is known from the outside; the mind (and culture) is understood from within. The methods of explaining na-ture are by analysis and experiment; mental and cultural phenomena are understood by means of "ideas" specially constructed to isolate significance for each other and for man. The neo-Kantians, on the other hand, also redivided the world of thought but in terms of whether reality is comprehended as history or as science. Be it physi-cal or psychological, science seeks to establish laws by means of experimental and mathematical-statistical analysis. History, how-ever, is the endeavor to comprehend and causally account for the unique and particular. It requires the employment of value concepts in terms of which alone the unique can be understood. Both the neo-idealistic and neo-Kantian thinkers tended to return to individu-alistic theories and analytical (rather than dialectical-synthetic) methods.

Such, in schematic outline, was the primary drift in Western thought from the period prior to the middle-class revolution to the early twentieth century. The rationalistic thought of the seventeenth and eighteenth centuries in prerevolutionary Europe was individual-istic in theory and analytical in method. In the postrevolutionary nineteenth-century world the pendulum swung the other way. The new national communities had to be consolidated. Thought (much of romanticism and both Hegelian and Marxian thought) was theoreti-cally collectivistic and synthetic in method. In the late nineteenth and early twentieth centuries during Max Weber's period, the pen-dulum swung back. New versions of theoretical individualism and analytical methods appeared. Weber was acquainted firsthand with Wilhelm Dilthey, a major neo-idealist, from his father's household. He was acquainted as a colleague and associate with such major neo-Kantians as Heinrich Rickert, Wilhelm Windelband, and Georg Simmel. He moved within the central drift of the times.

The Central Themes in Max Weber's Writing

Weber's writing may be divided into two great periods: the period of probing and experiment beginning with his Ph.D. dissertation and habilitation thesis (1897) and comprising various other essays and research reports to 1903; and the period beginning with the production of his essay on "Objectivity in Social Science and Social Policy" and the first part of his "Protestant Ethic and the Spirit of Capitalism," both of which were first published in the *Archiv für Sozialwissenschaft und Sozialpolitik* in 1904. The first period covered in Weber's investigations of and writing on German agrarian problems and the stock market. The second period coincided with his sufficient recovery from his nervous breakdown to assume the editorship of the *Archiv* and covers the unflagging productivity extending to his death. It was in the second period that he formulated the great themes for which he is famous.

Max Weber's Methodology

Max Weber's biography and his *milieu* cooperated to thrust him away from the kinds of methods associated with both right- and left-wing collectivism—that is, dialectical and synthetic methods. The starting point for Weber's analysis in this as in other cases seems to display a conservative bias. There is a strong tendency to start with the assumption that whatever exists is probably right and any problems are defects of one's personal perceptions. Weber's inclination, in short, is always to transpose problems presented by the external world into conflicts of conscience. Some of the characteristics of Luther's conception of the world as God's handiwork and of the individual's role as his "calling" persist in an otherwise secularized outlook.

Weber's essay on "Objectivity in the Social Sciences" is a kind of methodological testament at the point in his life when he was about to undertake a mature confrontation of his problems. It also belongs in the most intimate sense to the wave of thinking of the renascent individualism which swept Western culture in the late nineteenth and early twentieth centuries. The essay is characterized by acceptance of both the neo-Kantian and neo-idealistic methodological principles and the effort to compromise their difference while preserving their insights. The parallelism between various of Weber's formulations and those of Dilthey and Rickert may illustrate this.

The cultural sciences, Dilthey had argued, analyze their material from the inside on the basis of special interpretive constructs. They differ from the natural sciences which seek mathematical and experimental knowledge of nature. Science is science, Rickert had answered, whether its content be man or nature. If there are distinctions, they are methodological. Science, which is a search for nomological knowledge, should not be confused with history, which is concerned with the unique. Special methods are appropriate to the idiographic knowledge of history in contrast to those appropriate to the nomological knowledge of science.

Weber took over from Dilthey the methodological device of utilizing special interpretive constructs or ideal types. However, with Rickert he was inclined to treat all science as a single conceptual enterprise differentiated from history.

The aim of social science, according to Weber, is to understand "the characteristic uniqueness of the reality in which we move."[14] This type of historical understanding does not constitute establishing a system of laws. "As far back as we may go into the grey mist of the far-off past, the reality to which the laws apply always remains equally *individual,* equally *undeducible* from laws."[15] Socio-cultural analysis is concerned with configurations of factors arranged to form historically significant cultural phenomena. "Significance" is a value concept and the analysis of cultural science oriented to it involves a subjective element so far as it concerns events to which cultural significance is attached. Social psychological research consists of the study of many "*individual* types of cultural elements with reference to their interpretability by our empathic understanding."[16]

The type of concept construction indispensable to the cultural sciences, thus, consists, according to Weber, in framing the synthetic constructs or ideal types. Such ideal types are not hypotheses, though they may aid in framing hypotheses. "An ideal type is formed by the one-sided accentuation of one or more points of view and by the synthesis of a great many diffuse, discrete, more or less present and occasionally absent *concrete individual* phenomena, which are arranged according to those one-sidedly emphasized viewpoints into a unified *analytical* construct."[17]

Types do not supply ideals of what ought to exist but are ideal only in a logical sense serving to clarify analysis. The critical properties which remove the type from an evaluative ideal is the presence in it of relationships "which our imagination accepts as plausibly motivated and hence as 'objectively possible' and which appear as *adequate* from the nomological standpoint."[18]

Ideal types, Weber maintained, are intended for use in the analysis of "historically unique configurations or their individual components by means of genetic concepts."[19] They are indispensable for the obtaining of objectively valid empirical knowledge of social reality. "Nothing should be more sharply emphasized than the proposition that the knowledge of the *cultural significance of concrete historical events and patterns* is exclusively and solely the final end which ... concept-construction and the criticism of constructs also seek to serve."[20]

In Max Weber's methodological testament at the beginning of his great period of mature work, the methodological reflections of the neo-idealists and neo-Kantians were brought into synthesis with greatest emphasis on the latter. While Weber never completely retreated from this methodological stand in his later work, he was to modify it increasingly, viewing ideal typical procedures as instruments for achieving general (lawlike) knowledge of social events and not simply as devices for estimating the unique significance of special cultural configurations.

Max Weber's Theoretical Elementarism

The substantive work which opened the mature phase of Weber's productivity was *The Protestant Ethic and the Spirit of Capitalism.* The initial conservativism which so often led Weber to begin an analysis as if on the assumption that everything that exists is essential is manifest in the *Protestant Ethic.* In scientific circles in the late nineteenth and early twentieth centuries powerful antireligious currents were present. Furthermore, thinkers of a Marxian persuasion were inclined to dismiss religion as secondary to economic circumstances. Religion was an "opiate of the masses," serving to pacify them in the teeth of economic exploitation. Critical to Weber's analysis, however, was the recovery of a sense of the positive importance of religion for economics. This occurred despite his personal agnosticism.

To some extent the old polarity between Weber's parents, between a worldly father and a pious mother, may have been operating. Both attitudes were taken, so to speak, as indispensable parts of the whole.

Theoretically Weber's analysis of capitalism was elementaristic. He avoided analysis of capitalistic society as a whole or historical epoch or process, within which various forces are identified. Rather, Weber assumes that "capitalism" is no more than a name for a way in which some contemporary individual men behave. The critical questions then become: Who are the men who act in this peculiar way? What, precisely, is peculiar about the way they act? How could this way of acting have arisen?

A capitalistic economic action was defined by Max Weber as one which rests on the expectation of profit by the utilization of opportunities for exchange. Where rationally pursued, economic action rests on calculations in terms of capital represented by sytematic use of goods and personal services as means of acquisition to yield a net profit at the close of the business period.[21] Many forms of capitalism have developed but only in the West, according to Weber, have types appeared resting on the rational capitalistic organization of formally free labor. This, in turn, required the separation of business from the household and invention of rational bookkeeping.[22]

Weber maintained that the occupational statistics of any Western country of mixed religious composition show business leaders and owners of capital as well as higher grades of skilled labor to be predominantly Protestant. While a large majority of the wealthy towns of Europe in the sixteenth century went over to Protestantism, giving the Protestants an economic advantage, the linkage between Protestantism and capitalism is not to be explained simply by any such historical accident. For capitalistic economic behavior to arise, traditional forms of economic behavior had to be eliminated, and the Reformation helped in this. However, the Reformation did more than banish traditional controls by the church of everyday, including economic conduct; it created new and in many ways more burdensome systems of controls covering all phases of public and private life.

The peculiarity of the social ethic of capitalism, as Weber saw it, was the systematic rationalization of individual conduct whether such conduct involved employment of one's personal energies or only of his material possessions as capital. Systematic rationalization is a basic property of capitalistic economic behavior. "One of the fundamental characteristics of an individualistic capitalistic economy" is "that it is rationalized on the basis of rigorous calculation, directed with foresight and caution toward the economic success."[23] Its rational character differentiates capitalistic economic behavior from the subsistence activities of the peasant, the traditional economic behavior of the guild craftsman, and the type of capitalistic behavior of adventurers exploiting political opportunities or irrational speculation for profit. The sources of the spirit of capitalism, thus, must be found in those factors which led to the systematic elimination of traditionalism and the reorganization of everyday life on the basis of sober rational analysis. The origin of this kind of rationalization of life can be traced, Max Weber argues, to the religious idea of a "calling" and to the devotion of labor in a calling.

The conception of one's place in the world, one's calling, as a task set by God was a conception peculiar to the Protestant sects. For members in these sects it replaced the traditional concept of the monastery as the perfection of the Christian life. "The only way of living acceptable to God was not to surpass worldly morality in monastic asceticism, but solely through the fulfilment of the obligations imposed upon the individual by his position in the world. That was his calling."[24] This provided a moral justification for worldly activity. However, while he gave prominence to the idea of "calling," Luther's orientation toward everyday activity remained quite traditionalistic. His position on usury, for example, was much less favorable to capitalistic enterprise than that of the scholastics.[25] The Calvinistic interpretation gave the concept of calling its decisive form.

> The God of Calvinism demanded of his believers not single good works, but a life of good works combined into a unified system. There was no place for the very human Catholic cycle of sin, repentance, atonement, release, followed by renewed sin. Nor was there any balance of merit for a life as a whole which could be adjusted by temporal punishments or the Churches' means of grace. The moral conduct of the average man was thus deprived of its planless and unsystematic character and subjected to a consistent method for conduct as a whole.[26]

It was not Weber's argument that "the spirit of capitalism . . . could only have arisen as the result of certain effects of the Reformation, or even that capitalism as an economic system is a creation of the Reformation."[27] This Weber described as a "foolish and doctrinaire thesis." Rather, he argued only that religious forms played a part in the "qualitative formation and quantitative expansion" of the spirit or psychology of capitalism. In Weber's own summary: "One of the fundamental elements of the spirit of modern capitalism, and not only of that but of all modern culture: rational conduct on the basis of the idea of the calling, was born . . . from the spirit of Christian asceticism."[28]

Coming as it did at a critical time of his life, Weber's essay on the influence of the Protestant ethic on everyday conduct had many of the properties of a major act of self-clarification. For Max Weber was —and saw himself—as a particularly clear illustration of the Protestant ethic operating under circumstances from which—as in the cases of contemporary economic behavior—the specific religious content has melted away. In the essay he established the elementaristic orientation which remained basic to all his later work. The suggestion in the concluding paragraphs that the spirit of Christian asceticism fundamental to the ideal of calling was a basic component not only of the spirit of capitalism, but of all modern culture, is indicative of the extent to which Weber's imagination had already contemplated a program of possible scholarly investigation which could become coextensive with the range of human culture. Weber did in fact undertake the study of the rise and influence of rationalism in many other areas of life, such as in law, the state, and even in Western music.

Seen in this light, it is only a short step from the Protestant ethic to the general analysis of economic, political, legal, and cultural institutions of *Wirtschaft und Gesellschaft*. Moreover, Weber's extensive labors on the economic consequences of the religious ethics of other world religions (Confucianism, Hinduism, Buddhism, on which he was working in 1916 and 1917, and ancient Judaism on which he was working in 1918 and 1919) were a logical extension to complementary areas of the kinds of investigations undertaken in the *Protestant Ethic*.

The extent to which the kinds of problems and orientations established in the *Protestant Ethic* remained for the rest of his life is dramatically illustrated by the two famous addresses on "Science as a Vocation" and "Politics as a Vocation" delivered before the students' organization of the University of Munich in 1919. Both science and politics were approached from the standpoint of the concept of "calling" which had played the central role in the *Protestant Ethic*. It is noteworthy that Weber speaks of vocation of the scientist as if it were the last great heir of the Protestant calling. "Science today is a 'vocation' organized in special disciplines in the service of self-clarification and knowledge of inter-related facts. It is not the gift of grace of seers and prophets dispensing sacred values and revelations, nor does it partake of the contemplation of sages and philosophers about the meaning of the universe. This, to be sure, is the inescapable condition of our historical situation."[29]

Central to Weber's examination of the role of the politician in contemporary society are his contrasts between the political amateur (who lives *for* politics) and professional (who lives *off* politics) and the contrast between an ethic of absolute ends and an ethic of responsibility as alternative bases for political conduct. The formulations of this penetrating address may not unfairly be viewed as Weber's final estimation of the twin principles basic to the conflicts of his parental household: an ethic of absolute ends was implied by the attitudes of his pious, religiously oriented mother; an ethic of responsibility was implied by the attitudes of his pragmatic, politically oriented father. Weber saw the point of gravity of contemporary political life to be located in the political professional operating most effectively when, rising above principle, he seeks to discover a course that maximizes the values of all parties to the political act.

Who could doubt that for Max Weber at least his activity as a scientist had significance as a continuous effort at self-clarification?

Weber's Epitomization of His Method and of His Theoretical Concepts

By 1910 Max Weber's productivity was in full stride. In 1909 he accepted the editorship of the encyclopedic review of the social sciences, *Grundriss der Sozialökonomik,* agreeing to do the volume on *Economics and Society (Wirtschaft und Gesellschaft).* His contribution to the project occupied much of his time between 1911 and 1913. The manuscript included his *Sociology of Law, Systematic Sociology of Religion, Sociology of Music,* and *Sociology of Economics.* He also undertook a general restatement of his methodology and formulation of central categories of his thought in connection with *Wirtschaft und Gesellschaft.* His examination of the "Categories of Interpretive Sociology" constitutes Weber's own fullest formulation of his theoretical position.

In Weber's mature formulation of his methodological and theoretical point of view, his elementarism was made quite explicit. Sociology was defined as "the science which attempts the interpretive understanding of social action in order thereby to arrive at a causal explanation of its course and effects."[30] In this formulation the positions of the neo-idealists and neo-Kantians were at once smoothly joined. The very essence of social life (with the neo-idealists) was conceived as meaningful social actions which it was the task of sociology to interpret. However, Weber immediately went on to urge (with the neo-Kantians) that one was seeking by such interpretation a causal explanation of the course and effects of social action. It is notable in these formulations that the subjective intentions of social actors are neither conceived to be some sort of an epiphenomenon nor to constitute the sole and exclusive factor in interhuman acts.

Weber's Mature Methodology

With this definition of the task of sociology, the most fundamental of all methodological problems consists in the procedures for isolating and interpreting the subjectively intended meanings in social interaction and estimating their significance in determining the course of this interaction. Meaning, Weber observes, may be the actual meaning in an individual case, it may be the average meaning of a plurality of actors, or it may be a theoretically conceived pure type. The line between meaningful action and mere reactive behavior cannot always be sharply drawn. Much interaction (in this case of traditional or habitual behavior) is only marginally meaningful. If one asks the average man of most societies the meaning of religious rituals in which he routinely engages, he may only be able to answer vaguely. Moreover, many mystical experiences cannot be adequately communicated and are comprehended by the observer or scientist sympathetically or empathically if at all. At the same time, it is not necessary to have been Caesar to understand Caesar. There is sufficient parallelism in the range of experience of most people to permit them sympathetically to comprehend each other. Hence the interpretation of meaning which the sociologist attempts may be rational (logical, scientific, or mathematical) or emotionally empathic. When one formulates a mathematical proposition such as $2 \times 2 = 4$, this can be understood directly by anyone acquainted with the rules of arithmetic. But many religious, artistic, and emotional activities are understood by the imaginative participation of an individual in them. However, despite the fact that we rely on empathic sensitivity to estimate the meaning of many types of activities, for scientific purposes "it is convenient to treat all irrational, affectually determined elements of behavior as factors of deviation from a conceptually pure type of rational action."[31] Rationally pure types of action, however, do not represent judgment of social reality. They are methodological devices developed for convenience. In this sense only is the method of sociology rationalistic.

Many factors which have an influence upon social interaction (such as human mortality, the organic life cycle from infancy to old age, climatic and geographic factors, and so on) are devoid of meaning in that they cannot be related to action in the role of means or ends, but only constitute stimuli or favorable or hindering circumstances. Such nonmeaningful factors are often of greatest sociological importance. In the causal explanation of social phenomena these facts (including also psychic and physical phenomena such as fatigue, habituation, memory, states of euphoria, and the like) must be included. This does not, however, alter the central task of sociology of undertaking the interpretation of action in terms of its subjective meaning.[32]

Understanding in terms of subjective meaning may be direct and rational as when one understands an argument or logical demonstration directly in terms of the arguments supplied, or understanding may be explanatory in terms of motive. Explanations in terms of motive consist in placing the given act in a more inclusive context of meaning. Interpretation in terms of motive may be concerned with the intended meanings of concrete individual action, with average meanings in the case of sociological mass phenomena, or with meanings appropriate to a pure type. The interpretation of a subjectively intended meaning may be adequate on the level of meaning (when it corresponds to our habitual modes of thought and feeling) or it may be correct (when it can be shown to be not only adequate on the level of meaning but causally adequate). "The most perfect adequacy on the level of meaning has causal significance from a sociological point of view only in so far as there is some kind of proof for the existence of a probability that action in fact normally takes the course which has been held to be meaningful."[33]

Although it is often convenient to treat collectives such as states, associations, corporations, foundations, and the like as if they were individuals, for the subjective interpretation of action in sociological work such collectivities "must be treated as *solely* the resultants and modes of organization of the particular acts of individual persons, since these alone can be treated as agents in a course of subjectively understandable action."[34]

In these formulations Weber had not only brought the various elements taken from the neo-idealists and neo-Kantians into close formulation, but he shifted away from his earlier methodological position (formulated in the 1904 methodological essay) which would restrict sociological analysis to the estimation of unique historical cultural configurations. He now insisted:

> It has continually been assumed as obvious that the science of sociology seeks to formulate type concepts and generalized uniformities of empirical process. This distinguishes it from history, which is oriented to the causal analysis and explanation of individual actions, structures, and personalities possessing cultural significance. The empirical material which underlies the concepts of sociology consists to a very large extent ... of the same concrete processes of action which are dealt with by historians.[35]

Weber's Basic Conceptual Apparatus

The most fundamental of all concepts in Weber's sociology is that of social action. Social acts are taken as the atoms or elements of all social phenomena. Social action, including failure to act when this is intended and passive acquiescence, may be directed to past, present, or expected future behavior of others. Actions toward objects are not strictly social but have a social dimension so far as they are respected or taken into account by others. Not all contacts between persons are social. Contacts may be merely reactive as when two people jostle one another in a crowd. Needless to say, such jostling may give rise to social action. However, the fact that a number of persons act the same does not make it social; it may simply be the common reaction to some nonsocial stimulus (as in the case of much crowd behavior). Much imitative behavior may be only social in a borderline sense. However, "sociology, it goes without saying, is by no means confined to the study of 'social action'; this is only . . . its central subject matter, that which may be said to be decisive for its status as a science."[36]

For the analysis of social events into social acts, the most fundamental distinction lies between different types. Weber isolated four basic types of action in terms of the kind of relation holding between means and ends:

(1) in terms of rational orientation to a system of discrete individual ends (*zweckrational*); that is, through expectation as to the behavior of objects in the external situation and of other human individuals, making use of these expectations as 'conditions' or 'means' for the successful attainment of the actor's own rationally chosen ends; (2) in terms of rational orientation to an absolute value (*wertrational*), involving a conscious belief in the absolute value of some ethical, aesthetic, religious, or other form of behavior, entirely for its own sake and independently of any prospects of external success; (3) in terms of affectual orientation, especially emotional, determined by the specific affects and states of feeling of the actor; (4) traditionally oriented, through the habituation of long practice."[37]

In the end every sociological analysis consists in the determination of some one or some complex of these action types. It is noteworthy that Weber's *Protestant Ethic* reduces to a discussion of the manner in which actions of a *wertrational* type born in ascetic Protestantism eliminated traditionalistic actions and gradually generated economic actions of a *zweckrational* type. There is a clear progression in Weber's development from his 1904 essay to this theoretical formulation between 1911 and 1913.

Granted that the elements of social life are social acts, one must be able to deal with the behavior not simply of individuals but of pluralities, and one is particularly interested in the actions of pluralities that recur. The concept of "social relationship" was critical for permitting Weber to deal with such complexities and recurrences. "Social relationship" denotes the "behavior of a plurality of actors in so far as, in its meaningful content, the action of each takes account of that of

the others and is oriented in these terms."[38] A social relationship
from Weber's view consists exclusively in the probability that a
course of social action will occur. "A 'state' . . . ceases to exist in a
sociologically relevant sense whenever there is no longer a probability that certain kinds of meaningfully oriented social action will take
place."[39]

Weber's meaning can be clarified by taking social relationship to
refer to an interpersonal arrangement. For example, the interpersonal arrangement of dominance-submission requires at least two
persons. This arrangement may be present in a great number of
individual acts. However, the arrangement never exists *by itself*
apart from action. Hence Weber's argument that a social relationship
consists exclusively in the probability of the occurrence of certain
kinds of social actions. Nevertheless it is of analytical value to isolate
conceptually a social relationship such as dominance-submission,
since it identifies a recurrent form that may be present in a large
number of specific acts.

There are a number of empirical uniformities among social actions,
the types of which correspond to typically appropriate subjective
meanings attributable to the actors. An actually existent probability
of a uniformity of social action is a *usage.* Usage is *customary* if it rests
on long familiarity. Usage, however, may be purely rationally determined by employment of the opportunities of his situation in his self
interest by the actor. Usage is *fashionable* when the novelty of the
behavior is the basis for impirically uniform action by a plurality. As
distinguished from convention and law, custom refers to empirically
uniform actions not enforced by external sanctions.

Of particular importance for the formation of social actions involving social relationships into complex patterns is the existence of ideas
by social actors of the existence of a "legitimate order" of social
activities. The probability that action will in fact be oriented to the
notion that a legitimate order exists is described by Weber as the
"validity" of the order. A legitimate order consists in the recognition
by the actor of a system of maxims that are binding or that form a
desirable model for imitation. The fact that the person deliberately
subverts the order still involves his recognition of its legitimacy, as
when a thief through surreptitious acts acknowledges the validity of
the criminal law. Moreover, it is quite possible for a plurality of actors
to recognize the existence of contradictory systems of order both of
which are valid; an individual may act out of loyalty to his family, at
the same time acknowledging that his actions are violations of the
criminal law. There are four bases of the legitimacy of an order
corresponding to the four major types of social action: (1) because it

has been established in a manner recognized as legal; (2) because of rational belief in its absolute value; (3) by tradition and belief that it has always existed; (4) by virtue of affectual (especially emotional) attitudes legitimizing the validity of what is newly revealed or a model to imitate as occurs in cases of charismatic leadership.

Social relationships may be conflicting or solidary; they may be open or closed; they may be organized in terms of representation and responsibility, giving the actions of some persons consequences for others. Social relations are conflicting when oriented to the intention of carrying out the actor's will against the resistance of others. Conflict may be peaceable as in all forms of competition, or it may in varying degrees be warlike. Social relations are solidary or communal when based on the subjective feeling that the parties belong together. Communal relations, in turn, may be associative or affectual. Associative communal relations may correspond to the first two types of social actions (rationalistic and evaluative); solidary relationships usually rest on affectual or traditional bases corresponding to the second two types of social actions.

Social relations whether communal or associative are open when access to outsiders is not denied. They are closed when certain persons are excluded, limited, or subjected to conditions. Whether a relationship is open or closed may be determined expediently, rationally in terms of values, affectively or traditionally.

Finally, the order governing social relations may determine that actions of some persons have consequences for others. In the case of solidary members, all are held responsible for the action of any one. On the other hand, actions of certain members, the representatives, may be binding on the others. Representative authority may be completely appropriated in all forms, it may be conferred in accordance with particular criteria, permanently or for a limited term, or it may be confined to specific acts permanently or for a limited term, as in the case of appointment.

All these various kinds of social relations—conflicting and solidary, open and closed, representative and responsible—enter into the composition of a legitimate order. They are essential for the formation of noncorporate and corporate groups. The concept of the "corporate group" comprises a network of social relationships which are either closed or which limit the admission of an outsider by rules. When legally established, the order of a corporate group may originate by voluntary agreement or by being imposed and acquiesced in. The systems of order which govern corporate groups are "administrative orders" in contrast to the orders of noncorporate systems of action which may be described as "regulative orders." Corporate groups may be voluntary or compulsory. Among the central properties of the relations of individuals in corporate groups are power, imperative control, and discipline. Power is the probability that one actor in a social relationship is in a position to carry out his will despite resistance of others. Imperative control is the probability that a command will be obeyed by a given group of persons. Discipline is the probability that by virtue of habituation an order will receive prompt, automatic obedience on the part of a given group of persons.

An imperatively coordinated corporate group is political so far as enforcement of its order is carried out within a given territorial area by application of threat of physical force on the part of an administrative staff. An imperatively coordinated corporate group is hierocratic so far as enforcement of its order employs psychic coercion through distribution or denial of religious benefits. A hierocratic association with continuous organization is a church if its administrative staff claims a monopoly of the legitimate use of hierocratic coercion.

Such, in rather schematic outline, was the basic system of concepts ranging from social actions to corporate groups of the religious or political type by which Max Weber proposed to conduct his sociological analysis. The explanatory power of his formulations is revealed both in the great richness of his own studies and in the many researches by other scholars whom they continue to inspire. Nothing that could be said here can substantially add or detract from Weber's stature as one of the outstanding social scientists of all time. Here, for the moment, it is of more interest to note the element of human pathos never far from any of his work. This work always has the property of an act of passionate self-clarification. Always in the end there comes into view, behind his sweeping visions and enormous labors, the contours of a personality and career shaped in every detail by the Protestant ethic he so brilliantly described but operating in secular contexts from which religious hope has vanished. There remains only the lone individual condemned by the circumstances of his biography and *milieu* to bend every effort toward a salvation his mind cannot accept.

It was Max Weber's personal fate to feel compelled to transform all issues of the objective world into problems of his personal conscience. One is reminded of Nietzsche's famous passage on the madman who strode through the streets with a lantern at midday, crying that "God is dead. We have killed him." "Will we not," the madman had asked, "have to become like gods to be worthy of the deed?" It was Max Weber's personal destiny and, he thought, the destiny of all scientists to have assumed this God-like obligation, but with only the equipment of mortality for the task.

Notes

1. Daniel W. Rossides, "The Legacy of Max Weber: A Non-Metaphysical Politics," *Sociological Inquiry*, vol. 42, 3–4 (1972):183.

2. For example, "Borsengesetz" in *Handwörterbuch für Sozialwissenschaften*, 1st ed., supplementary volume, 1897.

3. H. Stuart Hughes, *Consciousness and Society* (New York: Alfred A. Knopf, 1958), p. 329.

4. Marianne Weber, *Max Weber: Ein Lebensbild* (Tübingen: J.C.B. Mohr, 1926), p. 249.

5. Ibid., p. 379.

6. Julien Freund, *The Sociology of Max Weber*, trans. Mary Ilford (New York: Vintage Books, 1969), p. 32.

7. Ibid., p. 288.

8. Ibid., pp. 32–33.

9. Ibid., p. 34.

10. Hans H. Gerth and C. Wright Mills, "A Biographical View," in Max Weber, *From Max Weber: Essays in Sociology*, trans. Gerth and Mills (New York: Oxford University Press, 1946), p. 11.

11. Ibid.

12. Freund, *The Sociology of Max Weber*, p. 33.

13. Weber, *From Max Weber*, p. 127.

14. Max Weber, *The Methodology of the Social Sciences*, trans. Edward A. Shils and Henry A. Finch (Glencoe: The Free Press, 1949), p. 72.

15. Ibid., p. 73.

16. Ibid., p. 89.

17. Ibid., p. 90.

18. Ibid., p. 92.

19. Ibid., p. 93.

20. Ibid., p. 111.

21. Max Weber, *The Protestant Ethic and the Spirit of Capitalism*, trans. Talcott Parsons (New York: Scribner's, 1930), p. 18.

22. Ibid., pp. 21–22.

23. Ibid., p. 76.

24. Ibid., p. 80.

25. Ibid., p. 83.

26. Ibid., p. 117.

27. Ibid., p. 91.

28. Ibid., p. 180.

29. Weber, *From Max Weber*, p. 152.

30. Max Weber, *The Theory of Social and Economic Organization*, trans. A. M. Henderson and Talcott Parsons (New York: Oxford University Press, 1947), p. 88.

31. Ibid., p. 92.

32. Ibid., p. 94.

33. Ibid., pp. 99–100.

34. Ibid., p. 101.
35. Ibid., p. 109.
36. Ibid., pp. 114–15.
37. Ibid., p. 115.
38. Ibid., p. 118.
39. Ibid., p. 118.

Selected Bibliography

English Translations of Max Weber's Writings

Ancient Judaism. Translated by Hans H. Gerth and Don Martindale. Glencoe: The Free Press, 1952.

The City. Translated by Don Martindale and Gertrud Neuwirth. Glencoe: The Free Press, 1958.

Economy and Society: An Outline of Interpretive Sociology. Edited, revised, and partly translated by Guenther Roth and Claus Wittich. 3 volumes. New York: Bedminister Press, 1968.

From Max Weber: Essays in Sociology. Translated by Hans H. Gerth and C. Wright Mills. New York: Oxford University Press, 1946.

General Economic History. Translated by Frank H. Knight. Greenberg Publishers, 1927; reprinted, Glencoe: The Free Press, 1950.

Max Weber on Law in Economy and Society. Translated by Edward A. Shils and Max Rheinstein. Cambridge: Harvard University Press, 1954.

The Methodology of the Social Sciences. Translated by Edward A. Shils and Henry A. Finch. Glencoe: The Free Press, 1949.

The Protestant Ethic and the Spirit of Capitalism. Translated by Talcott Parsons. New York: Scribner's, 1930.

The Rational and Social Foundations of Music. Translated by Don Martindale, Johannes Riedel, and Gertrude Neuwirth. Carbondale: Southern Illinois Press, 1958.

The Religion of China: Confucianism and Taoism. Translated by Hans H. Gerth. Glencoe: The Free Press, 1951.

The Religion of India. Translated by Hans H. Gerth and Don Martindale. Glencoe: The Free Press, 1958.

The Sociology of Religion. Translated by Ephraim Fischoff. Boston: The Beacon Press, 1963.

The Theory of Social and Economic Organization. Translated by A. M. Henderson and Talcott Parsons. New York: Oxford University Press, 1947.

Secondary Sources

Bendix, Reinhard. *Max Weber, An Intellectual Portrait.* New York: Doubleday Anchor Books, 1962.

Freund, Julien. *The Sociology of Max Weber.* Translated May Ilford. New York: Vintage Books, 1969.

Wrong, Dennis H. *Max Weber.* Englewood Cliffs, N.J.: Prentice Hall, 1970.

3

The Titans of American Sociology: Talcott Parsons and C. Wright Mills

Discussions of outstanding men often employ roughly defined categories of first-, second-, or third-rate minds or talents. These are not necessarily invidious distinctions. A first-rate mind is one which cuts through current stereotypes and finds its way to new solutions to social or theoretical problems. In his immediate social impact, a first-rate thinker is not necessarily as significant as a second-rate thinker, who is a person with sufficient ability to understand the creators and with the capacity to work up and systematize the new positions in formulations which make the new orientation available to the times. New messages often await for their social efficacy the discipleship of the second-rate thinkers. Third-rate scholars are characterized chiefly by the industry with which they transpose the formulas of the second-rate thinkers into stereotypes for routine exploitation.

In our time, for example, Talcott Parsons, the foremost macrofunctionalist, is such a first-rate thinker. Parsons has produced some three generations of students,[1] among whom are some[2] who have transformed macrofunctionalism into semipermanent form for routine exploitation. With considerable frequency Parsons has been adjudged the most significant professional sociologist in the United States in the post-World War II period. At the time of his death, C. Wright Mills, also among the first-rate sociologists of his generation, was evolving into Talcott Parsons' great rival. While his teaching was in the college rather than in the graduate school at Columbia, preventing him general participation in the training of neophytes, Mills also was developing a considerable following, and it has been estimated by some, particularly European, students that he was the most significant American sociologist of the postwar period.

The first-rate thinkers of a generation exist in varying grades and types. They may be major or minor (depending on the importance and scope of the assumptions they transform); they may be theory or action oriented. While neither Parsons nor Mills has the scope and theoretical intensity of a Max Weber, nor the revolutionary impetus of a Marx, Lenin, or Trotsky, there is little doubt that they are or have been among the first-rate thinkers of the current sociological generation. By the 1950s Parsons and Mills had emerged as the titans of American sociology. Both men began their careers as social behaviorists; both responded creatively to the formulas of their youth and worked their way to new positions; both became centers of new conceptual ferment.

The comparison of Parsons and Mills is of special interest, because with considerable frequency they have been taken as the major antagonists expressing the fundamental polarity in postwar sociological thought. While the dimensions of current social theory are not exhausted by the alternatives supplied by Parsons and Mills, this idea testifies to their influence. To recover the picture of the full richness of current theory, it will be necessary to take account of some things on which both Mills and Parsons, despite their many differences, are agreed, but which some other social theorists do not accept.

The personal evolution of a first-rate mind occurs only when the assumptions with which it was supplied by its teachers are not adequate to its problems. A peculiar kind of intellectual courage is required to question the assumptions of one's epoch—to face up to the deepest of all forms of spiritual uncertainties. It is as if the fixed stars have vanished from their places and the universe itself falls through an immensity. It is an experience most men cannot bear for long, for it is to be lost, not as an adult may be lost, in the unshaken conviction that there is a right way which only needs to be found, but to be lost in the manner of a child before the compass points of conceptual life have been fixed. It is to be lost absolutely or *in principle*—in a manner which erases the distinction between a right and a wrong way. When the fundamental assumptions of one's time are rejected, one comes face to face with *the ultimate relativity of all human ways of life. For at the base of every human way of life is not a given but a taken,* an assumption, an act of faith. At the moment doubt creeps into the act of faith on which a way of life rests, most men experience an extraordinarily intense need to deny the relativity of all specifically human ways of life. *At these moments it is necessary for men to create the gods to sustain the ways of life they have themselves invented.*

Career Comparisons: Mills and Parsons

Talcott Parsons, the elder contemporary of C. Wright Mills, was born of middle-class parents at Colorado Springs, Colorado, on December 13, 1902. Though sociology was not popular at the eastern liberal arts college to which he was sent, Parsons reports that it was here that he was converted to the social sciences as an alternative to biology and medicine.

> However, even though I was not introduced to sociology at Amherst, it was at Amherst I was converted to the social sciences. At the beginning the most important alternative was biology, and at one time I hesitated between biology and medicine. This beginning in biology has been an important influence ever since, and as an undergraduate I had a pretty good grounding in it. I was even an assistant in the laboratory of a general course in biological evolution, and I went for a whole summer to Wood's Hole, the famous marine biological laboratory.[3]

At Amherst Parsons reports among his most influential teachers Walter Hamilton and Clarence Ayers (who also influenced C. Wright Mills) and among the works to which he was introduced by these men were those of Thorstein Veblen ("for Veblen was an important mutual hero to both Hamilton and Ayers"[4]) which so impressed Mills as a young man as to lead his teacher, Hans Gerth, to say: "Mills came from Texas University with Veblen in one hand and John Dewey in the other."[5]

After graduating from Amherst in 1924, Parsons spent a year at the London School of Economics (1924–1925), where he studied with Hobhouse, Ginsberg, and Malinowski. While there he received a scholarship for study at Heidelberg (1925–1926), where he found an atmosphere dominated by the ideas of Max Weber who had died five years before. He received his doctorate from Heidelberg in 1928. From 1927 to 1931 Parsons served as an instructor in economics at Harvard. At Harvard, to which he had been invited to form a department of sociology in 1930, Sorokin reports that he rescued Parsons for sociology:

In December, 1930, I submitted the committee's plan for the department to President Lowell. He and the administration approved it with the exception of one point: they refused to approve the appointment of Talcott Parsons as the department's faculty instructor. Somewhat surprised by this, I asked Professor Burbank, chairman of the department of economics (where Parsons was an instructor) what could be the reasons behind this refusal. The gist of Burbank's remarks was that Parsons seemed to be less interested in economics than in sociology, that possibly for this reason his work in the department of economics was not of the best quality, that he probably would do much better work in sociology than in economics, and that therefore the department of economics would be only too glad to transfer Parsons to the new department. . . .

. . . I told Burbank that we were quite willing to have Parsons in the new department and asked him, Taussig, Gay, Carver, and Perry to support the committee's recommendation of Parsons to President Lowell and the administration. I also asked the members of the committee to exert all their individual influence upon the administration in this matter. Backed by their support, I did my best to convince Mr. Lowell to change his negative decision to a positive one. After two talks with Lowell I finally obtained his approval of Parsons' appointment.[6]

Some persons have been impressed by what they view as a weakness in Parsons' sociological roots: According to Edward Devereux Parsons not only "always regarded himself as something of a maverick in the field of sociology" but has been reproached for his disregard of the founders of sociology.[7] However, though rescued for sociology by Sorokin and originally displaying a thinness of anchorage in the historical names of the field, Parsons was destined to become the most powerful figure in professional American sociology in the postwar period. He was made instructor in sociology at Harvard in 1931, assistant professor in 1936, professor in 1939. He played a major role in the reorganization of sociology at Harvard which accompanied Sorokin's resignation as chairman. Sorokin describes these changes as follows:

Some four or five years later I asked again to be relieved from this position and was again refused. Finally in 1942, for the third time, I went to President Conant with this request, but this time I took with me a copy of the recent faculty vote on this matter. According to this mandatory vote, chairmen in all departments of Harvard should be appointed only for three years—in exceptional circumstances, for five years—and under no conditions for a longer period. Showing a copy of the resolution to President Conant I said that I had already carried on the duties of chairman for more than twelve years and that morally and legally I was entitled to be freed from these duties—the more so since, while I was anxious to be rid of the chairmanship, some other members of the department were very eager to attain this position. To my great satisfaction, this time my request had to be, and was, granted. This ended my responsibility for the department and its future development. *Nunc dimittis. Feci quod potut, faciant meliora potentes,* I said to myself lightheartedly after the release from these duties.[8]

Parsons was chairman of the department of social relations at Harvard from 1946 to 1956 and was elected president of the American Sociological Association in 1949.

While Talcott Parsons was raised as the son of a Congregational minister who later became the president of Marietta College, C. Wright Mills (1916–1962) was raised in a pious middle-class Roman Catholic family of Irish and English background. Mills' youth was spent in Sherman, Fort Worth, and Dallas, Texas, in which places his parents sent him to Catholic parochial and high schools. This was as natural for Mills' parents as for Parsons' parents to dream of an Ivy League education for their son. Mills' later career has been compactly summarized by his disciple, Irving Horowitz.

After an unpleasant year as an engineering student at Texas A. & M., he went to the University of Texas, where he received his B.A. and M.A. degrees in philosophy and sociology in 1939. With the exception of his election to Phi Beta Kappa, he did not participate in any of the usual extra-curricular college activities. From Texas he went to the University of Wisconsin, where, working under Howard Becker, he received his Ph.D. in sociology and anthropology in 1941. His teaching apprenticeship began at Wisconsin, where he held a teaching fellowship during 1940 and 1941. In 1941 he was appointed assistant professor of sociology at the University of Maryland; in 1945 he was for a brief time special business consultant to the Smaller War Plants Corporation, traveling and preparing a Senate committee report on *Small Business and Civic Welfare.* Immediately after the war end in 1945 Mills was awarded a Guggenheim Fellowship and also received an appointment as assistant professor of sociology at Columbia University. Until 1948 he was director of the Labor Research Division of the Bureau of Applied Social Research, where he worked under the overall supervision of Paul F. Lazarsfeld. After that, he remained at Columbia University in the department of sociology as an associate professor.

During his later years he held visiting lectureships at Brandeis University, the University of Copenhagen, the United States Air War College, and the William A. White Institute of Psychiatry. Mills retained the specifically anthropological capacity for researching people wherever the people were. He studied health needs for the Congress of Industrial Relations in Detroit, migration patterns of Puerto Ricans in New York, personal influence and mass communication effects on midwesterners. His later travels to Latin America and Europe assisted him in expanding his vision of the human mission of sociology. Thus he became acutely aware of the threat of thermonuclear warfare during his first visit to Western Europe in the early fifties, the dynamics of socialism in his later trips to Russia and Poland, and undertook to study the revolutionary process by going to Cuba at the time of Fidel Castro's emergence. This does not mean that Mills was simply a child of his experiences. It does mean that Mills' strongly pragmatic attitudes conditioned him to observe the social phenomena he was writing about.[9]

The parallelism between Parsons and Mills is rather extensive. Both men were raised in pious middle-class homes. Both came to sociology from other fields: Parsons from biology and medicine, Mills from engineering and philosophy. They shared an influence of Clarence Ayers, who introduced each to Veblen. Both men were attracted to institutional economics: Parsons through Walton, Hamilton, and Ayers, and later, by his teachers in the London School of Economics, Mills through Ayers and the atmosphere at the University of Wisconsin, where the most famous student of J. R. Commons (Selig Perlman) was at the height of his powers and where the traditions of Richard T. Ely, John R. Commons, and Wesley Mitchel were still fresh. Both Parsons and Mills were introduced to Max Weber: Parsons at the London School and later at Heidelberg, Mills at the University of Wisconsin, where Max Weber's theories were zealously promoted by Hans H. Gerth. Both men made their initial reputations with translations of Weber: Parsons with *The Protestant Ethic and Spirit of Capitalism* (1930) and Mills with his co-translation (with Hans Gerth) of selected essays from Weber: *From Max Weber* (1946). Both men were to make their way to positions of prominence in great eastern private universities.

Few people would dispute the proposition that by the 1950s Talcott Parsons and C. Wright Mills had achieved foremost positions in the respective spheres of sociology they occupied: Parsons in sociology's inner professional circles and Mills in its extra-professional relations with the wider learned world. Because of his position at Harvard, as chairman of the Department of Social Relations, and his semipermanent position in the professional society, Parsons developed a powerful network of ties to which he was key.

This was certainly the case with respect to Parsons' interactions with such colleagues and contemporaries as Clyde Kluckhohn in anthropology, O. H. Taylor in economics, or Samuel Stouffer in social relations. And it was still more the case in Parsons' relations with several

generations of junior colleagues and graduate students who sojourned
at Harvard, a changing group which in the first decade included such
people as R. K. Merton, Kingsley Davis, Robin Williams, and Wilbert
Moore, somewhat later included people like Marion J. Levy, Albert
Cohen, David Aberle, and Bernard Barber, and in the most recent
decade R. F. Bales, Edward Shils, James Olds, Renée Fox, and Niel
Smelser, to mention only a few.[10]

In the 1950s Parsons would almost instantly be named as the foremost sociologist of the United States, not only by members of the
profession but by most undergraduate students. On the other hand,
if one queried visiting foreign scholars and intellectuals in the mid-
1950s as to America's foremost sociologist, C. Wright Mills was almost
always named first. Parsons and Mills were the titans of American
sociology in the mid-century.

The Genesis of the Will to Succeed and Personal Style

There is a temptation to substitute a preoccupation with the human
foibles of outstanding men for the drama occurring in their minds.
The minds and often the personal lives of first-rate thinkers in all
fields are often rent by conflicts. It is impossible to imagine either C.
Wright Mills or Talcott Parsons rising to paramount positions in their
respective spheres without an extraordinarily powerful will to succeed. Each, moreover, has developed his distinctive personal style in
the course of his rise.

Too little objective information is available as yet to estimate with
any great hope of accuracy all the factors in the origins of the will to
power and the personal styles which carried each to the pinnacle of
his chosen sphere. Many persons other than Sorokin were impressed
by Parsons' drive to succeed, a drive which eventually drove Sorokin
to request relief from the responsibilities of the chairmanship at
Harvard.

> Morally and legally I was entitled to be freed from these duties—the
> more so since, while I was anxious to be rid of the chairmanship, some
> other members of the department were very eager to attain this posi-
> tion.[11]

At the time this author was a graduate student at Wisconsin, partly
overlapping Mills' career, he was impressed, as were others, by the
unusual power of his will to succeed. Dan Wakefield, who as an

undergraduate student at Columbia had been drawn to Mills' sphere by the magnetic pull of his charisma and who later became Mills' assistant and devoted follower, reports his mentor's preoccupation with success.

> "Now, Dan," Mills counseled me once . . ., "you're not married yet and you're living along. You must get one of your girls to come over every Sunday night and cook you a big stew that will last a week. You bottle it up in seven Mason jars, and take one out each day, and you have a good, healthy meal instead of that bachelor stuff." He was full of advice that was often valuable and always entertaining, from books I should read (he thrust James Agee's *Let Us Now Praise Famous Men* on me when it was out of print and not yet in vogue), to hints on work habits ("Set up a file"—and he showed me how), and running through all his advice was one grand theme, which served as his own motto, an approach to the world he called "Taking it big"—by which he meant subjects, and do them in the grand manner; a philosophy he not only preached but applied to everything from eating and drinking to writing. Almost any advice he gave ended with the exhortation, "Take it big, boy!"[12]

Wakefield was convinced that Mills shared the provincial's identification of "New York City as the citadel or Headquarters of Success." He described his mentor as an intellectual Gatsby, raised on middle-class success ideologies.

> I remember once driving with Mills from his house in Spring Valley to Columbia on a bright winter morning, and as we crossed over the George Washington Bridge, he pointed to the dazzling skyline and with a sweeping gesture said, "Take that one, boy."[13]

Harvey Swados, who perhaps knew Mills more intimately and for a longer time than anyone else, was impressed by the self-absorption associated with Mills' will to dominate. He reports that Mills seemed to have utterly no memory of the activities of others unconnected with his own.

> For many people this utter self-absorption was intolerable, and I must confess that there were occasions when it was for me also. But after a time it was borne in upon me that Mills could not function without the absolute conviction that what he was doing was not only right but was more important than what anybody else was doing. More than that, the unique thrust of his best work—I am thinking of the decade of the fifties, of *White Collar* and *The Power Elite*—derived directly from his egocen-

tricity. These books would have been paltry if they had not been informed throughout with a sense of the magnetic self-assurance of their author.[14]

Swados found a parallel "between Fitzgerald's crackup and Mills' terrifying conviction at the same age that he was written out, worked out, burned out."[15] Saul Landau, who met Mills and clung to him throughout his closing days, reports similar manifestations of a career dominated by a will to succeed which has reached its limits and experiences the backwash of depression when there is no longer any place to go.

> Mills embarrassed me into shaving my beard before we met Sartre and Simone de Beauvoir for lunch. He did it subtly so that I didn't realize exactly why I did it until a few weeks later. Anyway, his beard looked good. He resembled Hemingway, and although at first it was unintentional, he began to identify more and more with him. Hemingway had committed suicide a few days before and it shook Mills up. He talked about it for hours and then every day he would analyze it. It began, "obviously the man committed suicide. A man that knows weapons like he did would never point a loaded shotgun at his face. Of course he killed himself, the only way he could do it, with a hunting rifle. You know, that's the only way to do it; put the gun deep into your mouth and blast with both barrels. That's how I'd do it."
> I tried to change the subject and failed. "Look, he was used up. The man hadn't written anything for ten years. He was used out. What else was there for him to do? He had done it all, and he wrote himself out. That's me." And he laughed.[16]

But it is unnecessary to establish the presence of a powerful will to succeed in Parsons and Mills. The fact that each has achieved far more than many persons intellectually their equal if not superior to them is evidence enough. The problem is, rather, to account for the genesis of such drives and the form they assumed.

One may guess that the genesis of Parsons' personal impetus rests in part in his religious and family background. The son of a Congregational minister could hardly have been unaffected by the activational complex which, since Weber, has been described as the Protestant ethic. In its nonsacramental concept of religious salvation, Protestantism tended to cast the individual on his own resources, making him individually responsible for his religious fate. Wherever this orientation appears in pure form, it carries with it the tendency by the individual to turn his activities into a testing ground of his personal worthiness. Furthermore, the individual who practices such "inner-worldly asceticism" tends to measure his success in terms of objective achievement. Middle-class Americans living in a *milieu* once dominated by the Protestant ethic tend, in any case, to measure their successes in terms of achievement of their parents, and Parsons had as a personal standard a father who had made the ascent from the Congregational ministry to a college presidency. Whatever other things were operating, Parsons has shown the extraordinary capacity for hard work so typical of persons raised on the Protestant ethic, and his life also has borne the marks of an unusually intense demand for objective success.

Mills, too, may be assumed to have been personally paced by the demands for success, particularly objective success, characteristic of the American middle classes. However, Mills' drive did not possess the internalized form of an inner force in an upbuilding tension against internalized standards. His impetus was always directed outward as a rebellion against external obstacles. Despite the fact that his personal admirers, such as Swados and Horowitz, have not been impressed by the role of religion in Mills' motivations, his impetus has many of the properties typical of anti-clericalism and anti-authoritarianism. All his life Mills required external opponents: the middle classes, the power elite, and finally, anything American. One is tempted to guess that what began as anti-clericalism was successively generalized to more comprehensive contexts. Swados reports to have found in Mills

> ... a hatred, which became more ostentatious as the years went by, of everything marked Made in America. It seems to me that the last American vehicle he owned, before the MG, was that masterpiece of ingenious simplicity, the jeep.[17]

There is a close connection between the form of their respective drives, the spheres of their competition, and the personal styles of Parsons and Mills. Parsons' impetus seems to have been internalized as an up-building tension against mounting personal standards; Mills' impetus took the form of an ever more intense hatred of more and more generalized external opponents. Parsons was an in-fighter: in his department and in his university, in the official society, in the cliques of contemporary sociology. One of his long-time associates has described him as "the most masterful politician of contemporary sociology." Parsons' internal tensions led him to the psychoanalyst. Mills was a rebel against his department, against the professional society, against American society itself. Mills' personal tensions took him, not to psychoanalysists, but to the courts. His personal tensions exploded in a series of marriages and divorces and terminated in heart trouble and flight from the conflicts his actions generated.

> He hated the U.S., its politics, its culture, its "higher immorality." But he did not fit anywhere else, and he did not want to be anywhere else but in his own house, which he had built. It would be painful to be in the U.S. and read the *New York Times,* and face law suits, and petty professors writing personal attacks—to be in the same country that was preparing another invasion of Cuba, that would be testing bombs, and making counter-revolutions in little countries. Just reading the newspapers and not being able to do anything—it gave him chest pain.[18]

As a young man, when Mills had begun to undergo the first of his own troubles, he was fascinated by the personal problems of Charles Pierce. During the time he was a graduate student at Wisconsin, he felt a deep kinship with Pierce, not only because of Pierce's personal difficulties but of his empiricism as well. However, always in the end the personal lives of outstanding men are important for the light they may throw on the drama of their ideas.

The psychological foundations of the intellectual life of Mills have numerous superficial parallels to those of Rousseau. Like Rousseau, Mills' interests were neither purely theoretical nor purely practical. Like Rousseau, Mills was lionized by a society he despised. Like Rousseau, who worked out his intellectual destiny in the transition from enlightened individualism to romantic collectivism, Mills was gradually to abandon the individualistic social behaviorism of his early period for a collectivistic point of view. Like Rousseau's, Mills' style is often more clear than his thought. Like Rousseau, he was a slogan maker, capable of spinning out shibboleths calling diverse groups to common action. Finally, there is some evidence that, like Rousseau, Mills had an unusual tendency to project his personal problems into his intellectual ones, giving the drama of his emotions a universal scope.

The present volume is no place to trace all the points of intersection between Mills' personal problems and his theoretical concerns. Here they have interest primarily in accounting for the generation of his intellectual energies. The projection of his personal difficulties into his conceptual problems account, as with Rousseau, for the strident call to action which hovers in the background of all of Mills' formulations. One cannot but wonder whether, given the self-conscious choice, Mills would not gladly have supplied the program for a revolution in the twentieth century comparable to the manner in which Rousseau supplied the program for the French Revolution in the eighteenth. Perhaps this is why Mills, like Rousseau, appeals primarily to the young.

Mills' intellectual evolution, like that of Rousseau, has already been subject to uncertain and, at times, contradictory construction. Some of his critics, for example, have taken the position that he was basically a Marxist. This, indeed, was Parsons' judgment. Of current sociological theories other than his own, Parsons says:

> The types of alternative theory are . . . various, though probably a broad neo-Marxian type . . . is the most prominent. . . . Of the former type, such names as C. Wright Mills, Rolf Dahrendorf, Barrington Moore, and David Lockwood come to mind. . . .[19]

Since the publication of *Listen Yankee*, judgments as to the essential Marxism of Mills have become more frequent. At the same time, persons close to Mills have reported that he was taken aback at this misconstruction of this view.

If it is correct to estimate the personal styles of Parsons and Mills, respectively, as those of the astute political in-fighter on the one hand and of the rebel adept at guerrilla warfare on the other, it is quite impossible to imagine their success in spheres other than the ones they chose. Parsons' successes led him step by step to power within the profession; Mills' successes led him to ever wider audiences at home and abroad critical of one or another feature of American life. Characteristically, Mills' last truly sociological writing, *The Sociological Imagination*, before he departed permanently from its concerns, was a frontal attack upon what he viewed as all its main traditions. Swados seems unquestionably to be correct in sensing that Mills was set upon a course which involved ultimately the abandonment even of his professional role for that of sect leader. Mills, Swados urges, was entrapped by the temptation

> of being simultaneously a Teddy Roosevelt and a Scott Fitzgerald, a public figure—man of action and an artist-thinker. He was becoming a leader with a following. Not merely requests to speak, but pleas for guidance and counsel came pouring in on him, and after *The Causes of World War III* they became a flood. Under such circumstances the temptation to become oracular was almost irresistible; for a man who was absolutely sure of his own insight and analysis it was inevitable.[20]

The last days of the two types of figures bear some striking contrasts. After forty-two years on the Harvard University faculty, Parsons retired. In his note of the event in the *New York Times* Robert

Reinhold observed that while Parsons eschewed sermonizing his fellow men on the human predicament "both disciples and detractors would agree that no other living scholar has had more impact on modern social thought and theory."[21]

During the course of his service at Harvard, Parsons guided the careers of many leading sociologists such as Robert K. Merton, Kingsley Davis, Clifford Geets, Robert Bellah, Neil J. Smelser, Bernard Barber, Jesse Pitts, and Renée Fox.

Although retiring at the age of seventy, Parsons had no intention of departing abruptly from the halls of power.

> Retirement will not mean complete rest. He is in the midst of a major theoretical analysis of the American University as an institution, in collaboration with Gerald Platt of the University of Massachusetts.[22]

The last days of the rebel are another story. Swados has sensitively formulated the pathos that surrounded Mills' last days:

> I last saw C. Wright Mills in 1962, late in January, at the Nice Airport, where I had driven him from my French home so that he could return to America, after many months of fruitless wander about Europe, to die. His youngest child, who had been toddling about, tripped and split open his lip on the terrazzo floor. Mills was concerned, but unable to cope (fortunately his wife was). We shook hands, for the last time, and I looked back to see him walking slowly up and down with his child, being the dutiful parent because at this terrible moment he had nothing else to do with his time or with his life.[23]

Comparative Writing Styles of Parsons and Mills

One of the most immediately evident contrasts between Parsons and Mills appears in their writing styles. Parsons' writing has been found to be so complex and abstract, and to consist of so many finely interrelated distinctions that Parsons insisted were equally important, as to apparently defy summary and to lead many professional sociologists to renounce any claim that they could fully grasp his meaning.

The actual style difficulty may be illustrated by any passage taken at random from Parsons' writings.

> In one sense "motivation" consists in orientation to improvement of the gratification-deprivation balance of the actor. But since action without cognitive and evaluative components in its orientation is inconceivable within the action frame of reference, the term motivation will here be

used to include all three aspects, not only the cathectic. But from this motivational orientation aspect of the totality of action it is, in view of the role of symbolic systems, necessary to distinguish a "value-orienta-tion" aspect. This aspect concerns, not the meaning of the expected state of affairs to the actor in terms of his gratification-deprivation bal-ance but the content of the selective standards themselves. The concept of value-orientations in this sense is thus the logical device for formulat-ing one central aspect of the articulation of cultural traditions into the acting system.[24]

One may have to read this passage several times before one discovers that all it says is that "action involves values and ideas as well as pleasure and pain and the values are important."

By contrast one may consider a typical passage from C. Wright Mills:

The producer is the man who creates ideas, first sets them forth, possibly tests them, or at any rate makes them available in writing to those portions of the market capable of understanding them. Among pro-ducers there are individual entrepreneurs—still the predominant type —and corporation executives in research institutions of various kinds who are in fact administrators over production units. Then there are the *wholesalers,* who, while they do not produce ideas, do distribute them in textbooks to other academic men, who in turn sell them directly to student consumers. In so far as men teach, and only teach, they are *retailers* of ideas and materials, the better of them being serviced by original producers, the lesser, by wholesalers. All academic men, regard-less of type, are also *consumers* of the products of others, of producers and wholesalers through books, and of retailers to some extent through personal conversation on local markets. But it is possible for some to specialize in consumption. These become great *comprehenders,* rather than *users,* of books, and they are great on bibliographies.

In most colleges and universities, all these types are represented, all may flourish, but the producer (perhaps along with the textbook whole-saler) has been honored the most.[25]

One does not have to read this twice to discover that Mills is discuss-ing professorial writing and that he thinks it a rather crass commer-cial affair.

The passage by Parsons throws up a thorny set of apparently un-necessary complications. That by Mills hacks at its point with direct-ness and vigor. It was, perhaps, inevitable that the styles of these two giants of the 1950s and 1960s should so often be contrasted. Exposés of the pompous emptiness of Parsons' style have been carried out so often as to amount to a sort of intellectual parlor game by persons unsympathetic to sociology. With considerable unfairness it has often been suggested that Parsons' style is characteristic of what sociology "is," while that of Mills represents what it "ought to be." Yet, despite all its display of vigor, the passage by Mills says very little more than the one by Parsons. Mills has said only that "professors produce and consume books, and the producers have somewhat more prestige."

In the course of the many exposés of Parsons' writing, it has often been hinted that he could do no better and that the prestige of Harvard had permitted him "to get away with it." It is, of course, quite out of the question that a man of Parsons' brilliance could not have written more clearly if he chose. A man does not become one of the foremost members of a professional field without outstanding abilities. The hypothesis is offered here that Parsons wrote as he did by choice, that he developed a style as adapted to his purposes as was that of Mills to other objectives.

If one traces the source of the difficulties in Parsons' writing style, one is not long in discovering a few basic devices employed with infinite ingenuity to make the grasp of his meanings difficult. New terms are coined for familiar ideas. The writing is abstract, offering virtually no concrete illustration. Sentence after sentence, paragraph after paragraph, and page after page, indefinite references are pyramided in a manner which defies keeping track of the subject without special effort. The flow of the argument is continually being disrupted by independent and dependent clauses. That he knows what he is doing is shown by the fact that Parsons rarely ever loses track of his argument.

Parsons' writing style has been described by his disciples as architectoric. One can agree that his style has architectural parallels: it is medieval and defensive. It is not medieval gothic (with its synthesis of rational and sensuous values) which belonged to the city, but medieval domestic like the rural manorial architecture of the early Middle Ages. Just as the estates of a rural lord were protected by crude and apparently unordered but effective moats and baileys, so Parsons' meanings are endlessly guarded: by his special terminology, by indefinite references, and by parenthetical clauses. It is as if he were endlessly on the defensive from attack from every possible quarter. One can only grasp his meanings by marshaling his forces and laying siege upon endlessly varied, crude, but effective defensive traps.

If one once accepts the possibility that Parsons' style is not accidental but intended, a number of additional deductions may be made. It is unusually well adapted to an inner-professional strategy. Those who have not the capacity or endurance to make the assault upon its defense works and extract its meanings have no right to criticize. On the other hand, those who expand the extensive time and energy necessary to understand what is going on may not have learned anything very profound, but at least they have had a profoundly hard time getting there. And not many persons can admit after such expenditures of energy that it was not worth the effort. In any case, a subtle sense of profundity tends to cling to the writing simply because of the amount of effort required to master it. So successfully has his style served him that Parsons' critics have blamed the difficulty, the abstractness, and the obscurity of it not only on him but on sociology itself.

Closely tied to Mills' will to succeed was his preoccupation with self-presentation. As a graduate student at the University of Wisconsin he affected an air of breezy nonchalance of the kind that so impressed his followers later when his charisma was confirmed. He at times intimidated colleagues and teachers with a "bigger than life" illusion which Wakefield traces not only to his physical size—some six feet and two hundred pounds—but to his sense of restless energy and preference for unconventional dress.

> He commuted to Columbia in a rather bulky getup suggestive of a guerrilla warrior going to meet the enemy (which in a way he took the situation to be). He usually wore camping boots of some sort and either a helmet or a cap used for motorcycle riding, and was strapped around with army surplus duffel bags or knapsacks filled with books and notes.[26]

Mills' continued to behave at Columbia as he had as a graduate student teaching assistant at Wisconsin, at a time when other instructors wore a conventional white shirt, tie and jacket, while Mills lectured jacketless with an open collar, a wide belt, and motorcycle boots.

However, Mills' preoccupation with self-presentation from his graduate student days on was by no means confined to the cultivation of a distinctive physical presence. He was, if anything, even more concerned with his writing style. Even in seminar papers he shadowboxed with professional opponents as in a public forum. His two great style models of the period were Ernest Hemingway and Thomas Wolfe. He loved the terse impact of Hemingway and the force, like carefully aimed bullets, of his sentences. But he also liked the gusty rhetorical overflow of richness in Thomas Wolfe. In the long run, I felt he belonged more to Wolfe than to Hemingway because his genius, like Wolfe's, overflowed from a surging inner ferment.

Even in the early days it was possible to set down the principles which seemed to guide Mills' selection of devices which he began to weave into a style of his own: he was attracted by Veblen's rather pretentious academicism which in Veblen's hands was a means of heavy-handed sarcasm; he also was fascinated by the device which Dos Passos had borrowed from O. Henry and named the Camera Eye (the juxtaposition of apparently objective but carefully selected materials which give the lie to one another); and the device of Kenneth Burke of the transplanting of the language and images from an area where they originated to another (for example, using the language and images of war in the sphere of love or the language and images of love to describe warfare).

The language and imagery of the marketplace, for example, are employed by Mills in all sorts of areas and spheres one does not normally think of as commercial. Academic writers, for example, are described as producers, wholesalers, and consumers of books.

> Like the pharmacist who sells packaged drugs with more authority than the ordinary storekeeper, the professor *sells packaged knowledge* with better effect than laymen. *He brings to the market* the prestige of his university position and the academic tradition of disinterestedness.[27]

> In cafe society the major inhabitants of the world of the celebrity—the institutional elite, the metropolitan socialite, and the professional entertainer—mingle, publicly *cashing in* one another's claims for prestige.[28]

> One easily forgets that the under side of the glamour of cafe society is simply a service trade in vice. Those engaged in it—the procurers, the prostitutes, the customers, who buy and sell assorted varieties of erotical service—are often known to their associates as quite respectable.[29]

> Yet prestige is the shadow of money and power. Where these are, there it is. Like the national market for soap or automobiles and the enlarged arena of federal power, the national cash-in area for prestige has grown, slowly being consolidated into a truly national system.[30]

> Among those whom Americans honor none is so ubiquitous as the young girl. It is as if Americans had undertaken to paint a continuing national portrait of the girl as Queen. Everywhere one looks there is this glossy little animal, sometimes quite young and sometimes a little older, but always imagined, always pictured as The Girl. She sells beer and she sells books, cigarettes, and clothes; every night she is on the TV screen, and every week on every other page of the magazines, and at the movies, too, there she is.[31]

One can multiply the examples almost endlessly of the translations into the images and language of commerce of most diverse materials, always conveying the impression that one is dealing with a grubby, materialistic, despicable business—perhaps even worse than business itself, since it pretends to be something else.

While the style of Talcott Parsons is an instrument of defense, that of Mills is above all an instrument of offense. Parsons' style is calculated to hide its meanings behind an endless number of obstacles. Many a person has finally managed to surmount the obstacles and seize the meaning only to be informed by Parsons that he has advanced considerably beyond that position. Mills' style does not have to conceal its meanings, for it consists of demolition and assault devices intended to put its opponents in flight.

Personal Orientations to Western Cultural Traditions

No persons such as Parsons and Mills, arising to paramount positions in a major intellectual discipline of their times, can remain indifferent to its distinctive traditions. Every cultural tradition is distinguished by (1) its methods of analyzing the problems of man and society, (2) its modes of interpreting the relation of man to society, and (3) its strategies for realizing the good life. The distinctive methods of analyzing the problems of man and society in the West are the *humanistic* and *scientific.* The major interpretations of man and society are represented by *individualism* (which places primary emphasis on individual persons) and *collectivism* (which assigns primacy to society). Western individualism, in turn, is differentiated into *rational* and *nonrational forms.* Collectivism is subdivided into *right-* and *left-wing forms.* Individualism and collectivism are interpretations of man and his social life. *Liberalism* and *conservatism* are strategies for realigning the types of values made possible by social life.

As Parsons and Mills rose to their respective positions of eminence in inner- and extra-professional American sociology, they not only increasingly found themselves classified in terms of the structural features of the Western cultural tradition but found it necessary to locate themselves. To some extent the process of self-location was easier for Parsons. Since he has experienced himself and has been experienced by numerous others as representing the main stream of sociology, Parsons' task of self-orientation has primarily taken the form of locating his version of sociology. With respect to the primary value strategies of contemporary man (liberalism-conservatism), Parsons usually prefers to describe himself as a *liberal;* others, including many persons closely associated with him, describe him as a *conservative.*

The major act of self-location is accomplished by Parsons and his associates in the monumental *Theories of Society* of which he was senior editor. In this huge two-volume selection of pre-1935 sociological writings, all developments worthy of name are treated as an anticipation of the sociology of Parsons.

According to Shils, the sociology represented by Parsons "has come into its present estate because its own development bears a rough correspondence to the development of the consciousness of mankind in its moral progress."[32] Moreover, it "is not ... a purely cognitive undertaking. It is also a moral relationship between the human beings studied and the student."[33] However, while "the sociological theory that grows from the theory of action is simply a more forward part of a widespread consensual collectivity,"[34] Shils urges, "it is still the proud boast of some sociologists that sociology is an 'oppositional science.' "[35] Most of these, he suggests, are former or quasi-Marxists. They are said to focus on the miserable, the homeless, the parentless, the insulted and injured, and to generalize from them. They present an outlook "that radically distrusts the inherited order of society."[36]

While these formulations are Shils,' not Parsons,' the latter was senior editor of *Theories of Society* and permitted them to stand as a definitive summary of his position. Moreover, when an invitation was extended to Parsons in the Max Black symposium to defend his position, he formulated his views in a manner similar to Shils. Parsons showed somewhat more sympathy toward Marxism—at least the early Marxism of the 1890s. Early Marxism, Parsons observed, was an advance over the views that preceded it. However, Marxism, in Parsons' opinion, has in turn been superseded and, because of both its materialistic bias and its lack of differentiation, it is insufficient for dealing with the great problems of culture, personality, and social system in our day. Only the theory of action, that is, his own theory, is adequate to the task of contemporary analysis.

> It is my own profound conviction, which I both believe and hope to be justified, that the developments under discussion in this volume are deeply rooted in the main trends of the intellectual developments of our age. Their base-line of reference is a great synthesis which was achieved in the generation preceding ours—as the editors of *Theories of Society* have placed it, roughly 1890–1935.[37]

Parsons' concurrence in the judgments of Shils is quite complete. Parsons and his associates consider their form of sociology to be a "new foreward part of a widespread consensual collectivity," and the chief hope of mankind against all "alienated" positions such as Marxism which distrusts traditional society.

In his last works Mills, too, increasingly felt the need to locate himself in the historical traditions of the West. His genius was not one for the handling of pure ideas. One cannot ask of him the careful examination of intellectual traditions, even those he claimed most completely as his own. Nevertheless, in his last works, which are at once his most creative and controversial, various of the Western intellectual traditions within which and in part against which he was working had become so important to him as to lead him to various formulations concerning them. From *Images of Man* to the *Marxists*, one or the other of the traditions of the West was never far from the center of his reflections.

As intellectual history, the various presentations by Mills of the Western traditions are seriously inadequate. In his edited volume of classical sociology, he set down what he considered to be the essence of its classical tradition:

> No one, I believe, has stated better, or more clearly, than did the com-
> pany of thinkers presented in this volume the basic conceptions or
> theories of such matters as social stratification and political authority, of
> the nature of bureaucracy and of capitalism, of the scale and drift of
> modern life, of the ambiguity of rationality, of the *malaise* individual
> men so often feel.[38]

Mills' selection rigidly followed this proposal. He divided his treatment into three parts: "the first . . . concerns the difficulties of thinking clearly and well about man and society" (illustrated by selections from Walter Lippmann and Spencer);[39] "the second . . . suggests the variety of elements that go to make up a society" (illustrated by Marx's and Engels' concepts of class and historical materialism and by Mosca, Michels, and Pareto's concepts of the *élite*);[40] part three "contains several of the original . . . statements of the crisis of individuality" (illustrated by selections from Thomas and Znaniecki on personality, Simmel on the individual in mass society, and by Durkheim on anomie, by Marx on alienation, and by Mannheim on rationality).

These are vital modern themes, though the particular writers and selections chosen do not always represent the best statement of them. However, to take this selection of writings as the most essential examples of historical sociology and as a statement of its most vital problems is at least as one-sided as the two volumes, *Theories of Society*, edited by Parsons and others. In the Parsons' treatise a large number of fragments from pre-1935 sociology had been treated as anticipation of the writings of Talcott Parsons which, in turn, were presented as the solely significant sociology of the present. Again a striking similarity appears between Parsons and Mills, in that each conceives the sole value of historical sociology to be the anticipation of himself.

In his last work, in press at the time of his death, Mills attempted to delineate Marxism in terms of various thought movements. As he saw them, the two positive intellectual traditions of the West are Marxism and liberalism.

> In their classic versions, liberalism and Marxism embody the assurances and hopes, the ambiguities and fears of the modern age. They . . . constitute our major, even our only, political alternatives.[41]

Their common opponent is conservatism.

> In the United States . . . conservatism offers only a retrogressive utopia to circles best described as cranky, if not crackpot. Insofar as it is not that, conservatism is a defensive gesture of businessmen and politicians who would defend the *status quo,* but who are without ideas with which to do so.[42]

There is a notable failure by Mills to isolate conservatism as a value orientation from various political and social groups branded by the term and a failure to acknowledge the quite genuine values (social stability, peace, security) which lie at the heart of the conservative orientation. One may, of course, believe that social harmony is not enough and not worth the sacrifice of individuality, but that is another story.

Finally, Mills' failure to isolate distinct idea configurations may be illustrated by his derivation of Marxism and liberalism.

> Both Marxism and liberalism embody the ideals of Greece and Rome and Jerusalem: the humanism of the Renaissance, the rationalism of the eighteenth century enlightenment. . . . What is most valuable in classic liberalism is most cogently and most fruitfully incorporated in classic Marxism. . . . Hence to confront Marx and Marxism is to confront this moral tradition.[43]

The methodological positions which have emerged at the core of Western thought and the primary strategies of social life (individualism and collectivism) and their sub-forms (rational and nonrational individualism and right- and left-wing collectivism) illustrate the confusions which arise in the assignment to Marxism of the best of humanism, liberalism, rationalism, and the ideals of Greece, Rome, and Jerusalem. Some of Mills' attributions are doubly confusing, since there are both individualistic and collectivistic interpretations of Christianity and Judaism. One cannot know without specification what is intended by the assertion that their best traditions have been incorporated in Marxism.

Neither Parsons nor Mills presents a very accurate account of historical Western culture or historical sociology, though Parsons is rather more accurate than Mills. Parsons defines his position in terms of the inner structure of the field; Mills' problem was more difficult, for he had to define himself in opposition to a variety of positions. While Parsons liked to call himself a liberal, it is quite evident that anyone who views his position as "a more forward part of a widespread consensual collectivity" and is opposed to all positions that "distrust the inherited order of society," basically views himself as having a vested interest in the *status quo* justifying the attribution of conservatism.

Parsons' theories are no longer as popular with sociologists as they once were. Young sociologists particularly shun abstract theory in preference for immediate issues which they view as relevant. In stressing the tendency of social systems to resist change, Parsons is visualized as politically conservative. Situations of confrontation and conflict impress the young, rather than situations of accommodation and equilibration, as where the action is. However, though declining in size there remains, according to Reinhold, a circle that is loyal to Parsons.

Friends contend it is unfair to say that Talcott Parsons has removed himself from worldly affairs or that he is conservative. They note his strong stand against Naziism and McCarthyism, and the constant unselfish devotion, both from himself and his wife, Helen, lavished on a long parade of students.[44]

Mills, for his part, left no doubt as to his self-classification among those whom Parsons and Shils described as "oppositional" and "alienated." Mills' opposition to Parsons was direct and emphatic.

Is grand theory, as represented in *The Social System*, merely verbiage or is it also profound? My answer to this question is: It is only about 50 per cent verbiage, 40 per cent is well known textbook sociology. The other 10 per cent, as Parsons might say, I am willing to leave open for your own empirical investigations. My own investigations suggest that the remaining 10 per cent is of possible—although rather vague—ideological use.[45]

Apart from Parsonian theorizing, Mills maintains, sociological research is dominated by "abstracted empiricism" in which "the thinness of results is matched only by the elaboration of the methods and the care employed."[46] Mills illustrates what he views as its triviality by the World War II American soldier researches directed by the late Samuel Stouffer.

> These studies, it seems to me, prove that it is possible for social research to be of administrative use without being concerned with the problems of social science.[47]

So far as it is concerned with practical problems, contemporary sociology is characterized by "a new illiberal practicality."

> New institutions ... in which this illiberal practicality is installed: industrial relations centers, research bureaus of universities, new research branches of corporation, air force, and government ... are not concerned with the battered human beings living at the bottom of society —the bad boy, the loose woman, the migrant worker, the un-Americanized immigrant. On the contrary, they are connected, in fact and in fantasy, with the top levels of society, in particular, with enlightened circles of business executives and with generals having sizable budgets.[48]

Thus the self-locations of Parsons and Mills place them respectively in the positions of primary heirs and defenders of the sociological and social *status quo* on the one hand and the guerrilla leader laying siege upon these strongholds of "conservatism" on the other. This appears to cast Mills in the camp of the Marxists, but to the end he resisted any complete identification with Marxism.

The First Phase in the Intellectual Development of Parsons and Mills

Though Mills was fourteen years the junior of Parsons, both came to maturity in the interwar period: Parsons in the late twenties and early thirties; Mills in the late thirties and early forties. Despite different religious backgrounds, both came from middle-class strata of the American West. In this period the dominant politico-economic philosophy was laissez-faire. The counterpart of laissez-faire economic doctrines in American thought was pragmatism. While accepting, by and large, the individualistic values and suppositions of laissez-faire, institutional economics represented the beginnings of a critique of them. Both Parsons and Mills, as has been noted, were influenced as young men by institutional economics and by pragmatism.

American sociology in the interwar period had its strongholds in the midwestern universities: at Chicago, Minnesota, Wisconsin, and Michigan. Its strongest theoretical orientations in this period were various forms of social behaviorism: symbolic interactionism and pluralistic behaviorism. Symbolic interactionism was powerfully influenced by pragmatism. Pluralistic behaviorism was strongly influenced by individualistic traditions in Europe stemming from Gabriel Tarde. Also in the American midwest other European individualistic traditions represented by formalism found a ready reception.

Both Talcott Parsons and C. Wright Mills opened their intellectual careers as adherents of social behaviorism. It was perhaps inevitable that Parsons and Mills should begin from the same basic position in view of their class derivations, the dominant *milieu* in American thought at the time, and even the particular influence on each. However, both responded to social changes in their time and played a role in transforming the intellectual climate with which they were in interaction. These responses set them on divergent courses.

Parsons' First Phase: Student Days to 1939

Having been raised in the home of a Congregational minister turned college president, Parsons was directly influenced by an atmosphere in which the Protestant work ethic was an everyday reality. When he encountered Max Weber's tradition during his days at Heidelberg and read Weber's famous work, *The Protestant Ethic*, one can well imagine that a good deal of personal and public experience seemed to be synthesized by it. His translation of it effectively opened his intellectual career. Parsons observes:

> The first thing of his I read was the essay, *The Protestant Ethic and Spirit of Capitalism* (1904–5), and it was not altogether a matter of chance that a few years later I translated it for an English language edition. This essay, along with Weber's more comprehensive comparative empirical and theoretical works, has remained a very dominant influence on me.[49]

Parsons came to full stature as a significant contemporary sociologist with his first original book, *The Structure of Social Action*.[50] It consisted of a review and an attempt at integration of the theories of Alfred Marshall, Vilfredo Pareto, Emile Durkheim, and Max Weber. This was not an easy task, since Pareto and Durkheim are organicists with collectivistic analyses of social events; Marshall and Weber are social behaviorists with individualistic analyses.

The two major points in Parsons' first system of sociology which cannot be reduced to Max Weber's form of social behaviorism are his rejection of the positivistic analysis of social action (his assignment to social behaviorism properties which resist naturalistic analysis) and his insistence that systems of social action acquire emergent properties not reducible to the units and acts which compose social systems.

> To carry unit analysis to the point of the conceptual isolation of the unit act is to break up the system and destroy this emergent property.[51]

In his first work the foundation was already being laid by Parsons for a possible departure from Weber's type of social behaviorism.

Mills' First Phase: Discovery to 1947

The early stages of the formation of Mills' views were clearly a period of discovery for him. Contrasting positions were held simultaneously as appropriate to different sides of his interests. Mills was moved by a powerful reformist drive; he was a self-avowed socialist and follower of Marx. At the same time he was strangely insensitive to the Stalinist-Trotskyite controversy which raged in left-wing student circles. Mills was an old-line Marxist and Norman Thomas a socialist in his orientation to social problems.

Theoretically, of course, Marxism is a form of scientifically oriented left-wing collectivism. The units of social life are not individuals but social classes. Individuals only achieve significance for Marxism when they act in, and in terms of the requirements of, social classes. Moreover, this left-wing collectivism was conjoined to scientism and progressivism. Marxism was optimistic and sustained by the conviction that underlying the development of classes is an even more efficient application of scientific technology to the mastery of nature. In the end, despite all counter-revolutionary activity, scientific technology drives men through the conflicts which usher in the classless society and the utopian fulfillment of history.

While Mills at this time subscribed to a collectivistic approach to social reform, he simultaneously held a social behavioristic theory of social phenomena. His social behaviorism was, in part, derived from the pragmatic orientations he brought with him to the University of Wisconsin. It was further strengthened by the pragmatism of John Dewey which dominated the University's philosophy department.

At this time Mills also was influenced by Veblen and introduced by Hans Gerth to the social behaviorism of George Herbert Mead and Max Weber.

Through all forms of social behaviorism runs a strong clear vein of individualism. Veblen, Weber, and the pragmatists were, at times, socially critical, but they were also anticollectivistic. The units of social life were actions. Social groupings of all sorts (including classes) are not new kinds of entities with greater importance than individuals, but social strategies of pluralities. The Marxian theory of history tends to dissolve in their analyses into a maze of now larger, now smaller encounters of individuals and cliques and organizations.

The main impetus, more unconscious than conscious, of Mills' intellectual life in this period was the search for a formula which would fuse the Marxian and social behavioristic positions. The point at which they seemed to be common appeared to be that both were to some extent socially critical. That they presented different critiques with quite distinct consequences was passed over in silence. Characteristic of the lines along which such fusion tended to occur was Mills' modification of the social behavioristic theory of motivation in a manner which transposed it into general social-critical form. This was first worked out in articles and eventually transplanted to *Character and Social Structure,* written in collaboration with Hans Gerth.

Since Mills was fundamentally concerned throughout his career with the place of the individual in the social order, his conception of the individual lies at the very core of his interests. His contributions to the theory of motivation belong to his first, most purely individualistic, rationalistic, and scientific phase. His handling of the problem, however, demonstrates how uneasily he wore the mantle of individualism.

> Motives are generally thought of as subjective "springs" of action. . . . But there is another way to think of them. . . . We may consider motives as the terms which persons typically use in their interpersonal relations.[52]

> Sociologically . . . a motive is a term in a vocabulary which appears to the actor himself and/or to the observer to be an adequate reason for his conduct. . . . Conceived in this way, motives are acceptable justifications for present, future, or past conduct.[53]

> When a person confesses or imputes motives . . . he is . . . usually trying to influence others.[54]

> No one vocabulary of motives is accepted by everyone, so the alert individual must use one or the other tentatively, until he finds the way to integrate his conduct with others, to win them as allies of his act.[55]

The terms which the person uses to refer to his own feelings are socially confirmed by their use by other persons. Self-knowledge that is not socially confirmed, not yet disciplined by interaction with others, is not secure knowledge.[56]

As shocking as Mills would have found this characterization, he leaves little doubt that to him the problem of motivation concerns not the inner person (who, Mills argues, achieves reality only when his personal terms are confirmed by others) but interpersonal strategies. Vocabularies of motive are implements of social influence.

Even at this early stage in his thinking, Mills was in flight from social behaviorism. His treatment of motivation is not the argument of a man who will eventually assign, with Weber or Veblen or Mead and the other pragmatists, primary reality to the individual. The core of individuality was being hollowed out and assigned only schematic significance. Mills was in evolution away from social behaviorism, for even at this stage he was beginning to visualize individuality as a dangerously chaotic principle.

Parsons and Mills first established their intellectual orientations as social behaviorists. Each, however, shows the response and partial reception of collectivistic elements: scientific socialism in the case of Mills, the organismic sociology of Pareto and Durkheim in the case of Parsons. Ironically, in the first stage of their development Parsons showed a strong resistance to the positivistic (scientific) traditions in social science, while Mills identified himself with the ultra-positivistic philosophy of Charles Pierce. In his insistence that systems have emergent properties not reducible to unit acts, Parsons began showing signs of resistance to social behaviorism comparable to that of Mills in his early distrust of individualism.

Transitions in the Theories of Parsons and Mills

Talcott Parsons: Phase II

The possibility was already laid down in *The Structure of Social Action* for a departure from its confines. There are some indications that as early as 1939 preparation for this departure was already under way. In any case, by the time of his essay on sociological theory for the symposium of George Gurvitch and Wilbert E. Moore, the modification of his earlier social behaviorism was occurring.

In his second phase Parsons was inclined to break with various nominalistic elements in his earlier formulation. He became somewhat more critical of the theories of Max Weber than he had been earlier, somewhat more sympathetic with those of Durkheim. The primary task of sociology was no longer located in the analysis of social action, but in the analysis of the interrelation of institutions. Parsons was beginning to suggest that sociological analysis ought to proceed from the standpoint of the whole. This phase of Parsons' work falling between 1939 and 1949 displays a strong thrust toward a realistic position and a growing sympathy with positivism.

C. Wright Mills: Phase II

It is interesting to speculate as to how the second phase of Mills' work will eventually be viewed. At present any estimate is difficult, for his ultimate importance depends upon what happens to the traditions with which he worked. If the work in Mills' third and final phase becomes, as it could, the starting point for a new theory of sociology, his ultimate importance will undoubtedly be that of a creator and pioneer of new orientations. However, if it does not, Mills' significance will be found in his second period, in which he will be viewed not as a founder of new traditions but as an elaborator and interpreter of established views.

The central factor in Mills' second period consists in the carrying through of the program which was only envisioned in his student and immediate post-student days—the attempt to integrate the traditions of old-line Marxism and socialism with those of social behaviorism. This took the form of a review of the central problem of the left-wing collectivists (the problem of classes) in terms of the new tools of the social behaviorists (Veblen and Weber particularly).

Three major books belong to this period of Mills' development: *The New Men of Power, White Collar,* and *The Power Elite.* In these volumes three essentially socialistic themes were taken up and dressed in new terminologies. *The New Men of Power* rests on the Marxist and socialistic thesis that those persons who use the tools of production and their leaders hol l the future in their hands. In *White Collar* the Marxian thesis that as the final phases of the class struggle draw near the middle classes will wither away is reviewed and modified by tracing the rise of the new white-collar workers. The volume opens with the apocalyptic vision of their powerlessness. The impotence and shallow pretensions of the new middle classes are developed in terms borrowed from Veblen's theory of conspicuous consumption. The implication for the new middle classes is that they must either join the group that holds the future in its hands or become lackeys of powers that will exploit them. Finally, in *The Power Elite* the old socialistic and Marxian vision of the *bourgeoisie* exploiters of contemporary society is restored to its old position. Instead of capitalistic exploiters, the ruling strata are described as a *power elite*. However, the old evil vision of a conspiracy at the top remains. Weber's concepts of class, status, and power are employed as tools of analysis in this book in somewhat the same manner as Veblen's ideas of conspicuous consumption were employed earlier.

In Mills' second phase, as in the case of Parsons, the continuing modification of social behaviorism with collectivistic perspectives is obvious. Mills was showing an increasing tendency to reduce materials drawn from Veblen and Weber to "tools of analysis," while the substantive theories of social life to which he subscribed were increasingly drawn from left-wing collectivism.

The Period of Fulfillment: Parsons and Mills

Talcott Parsons: Phase III

It is a matter for speculation whether the rapid evolution of Parsons' thought from an individualistic to a wholistic form may not have been considerably related to the role of Pitirim Sorokin at Harvard. Sorokin has made an interesting case for this.

> Reading *Toward a General Theory of Action,* especially its most important part: "The General Theory of Action" representing the collective work of all the participants of the volume: T. Parsons, E. A. Shils, G. W. Allport, C. Kluckhohn, R. A. Murray, R. R. Sears, R. C. Sheldon, S. S. Stauffer, E. C. Tolman; and then reading T. Parsons' *The Social System,* I was pleasantly surprised at finding the readings in some parts easy and feeling myself in these parts pasturing on very familiar grounds. The more I read these works, the more familiar I felt, at least in their basic conceptual framework and in their main concepts. Soon I discovered the reason for this familiarity. It was a striking concordance between the basic conceptual scheme of the authors and my own conceptual framework. In a preliminary form my sociological framework was published first in my Russian two-volume *System of Sociology* (1921). In its fully developed form I have been hammering it in my courses at the Universities of Minnesota and Harvard since 1928; and since about the same time in several of my publications. Finally, it was published in its final form in first three volumes of my *Social and Cultural Dynamics* (1937) and then in its fourth volume (1941). Then it was reiterated in an abbreviated form in my *Sociocultural Causality, Space, Time* (1943) and in my *Society, Culture, and Personality: Their Structure and Dynamics* (1947). . . .
> While there is a multitude of dissimilarities between two conceptual

systems, there is hardly any doubt that the basic framework of the authors exhibits a notable resemblance to my framework.[57]

Following this statement Sorokin presented some eight-and-a-half single-spaced pages of comparisons between key notions from Parsons' works and his own of earlier publication. Sorokin stated in summary:

> The total body of these similarities is so evident that though my theories are neither mentioned nor referred to in both volumes, I contend that none of the numerous theories gratefully mentioned by the authors (M. Weber, V. Pareto, S. Freud, E. Durkheim, L. Henderson, and others) are so similar to the framework of the authors' as the conceptual framework developed—logically and empirically—in my courses and publications. Even more, there is no sociological, anthropological, or psychological theory in the whole field of psychosocial sciences as similar to the basic conceptual framework of two volumes discussed as my framework or, more exactly my re-formulation, development and test of the theories of many earlier eminent social thinkers. The basic framework of the new volumes is notably different even from that of T. Parsons' *Structure of Social Action.* His new framework shows a very tangible departure from the semi-nominalistic and singularistic standpoint of the *Structure of Social Action* with its main axis of the "means-end-schema." Now this standpoint and schema are practically abandoned in favor of "a more generalized level" of analysis (S.S., 9) and the Weberian semi-nominalistic and singularistic framework of "actions," "actors and roles" is embraced by a more adequate "realistic standpoint" of "social system," "cultural system" and "personality system," or by the larger framework of "the whole play" in which "roles, actions, and actors" are but components. This shift explains why Parsons' present framework is more similar to my basic system than to that of his *Structure of Social Action.*
>
> Side by side with the basic similarities there is a multitude of dissimilarities between two sociological theories compared. These dissimilarities concern though important but mainly secondary points. Among many factors for these dissimilarities, one is due to Parsons' uncompleted transition from his previous standpoint to the new one. For this reason "the sins" of the previous framework continue to visit upon, to crop in, and to vitiate the new framework. Hence a peculiar eclecticism of his new standpoint. The incompatible elements of two different frameworks, put together, clash and do not allow a consistent logical integration into one system. They fill the new basic framework with many "logico-meaningful congeries." It is earnestly hoped that the transition will eventually be completed and will lead to an elimination of these congeries.[58]

Quite apart from possibly establishing the influence of Sorokin's "wholism" on Parsons, Sorokin's statement has interest in independently documenting Parsons' transition from individualism to collectivism. Sorokin also independently confirms the conflict of points of view which marks the transition period in Parsons' theories and which, as he indicates, persists into the third phase of Parsons' work.

Sorokin's conclusion to a parallel discussion in *Sociological Theories of Today* is an excellent summary of Parsons' development in his third phase: an increasing abandonment of the individualism and atomism of his earlier period and the integration of its form of wholism or functionalism. Parsons, for his part, has come quite explicitly to visualize his views as a form of collectivism.

> Parsons' new framework shows a very tangible departure for the seminominalistic and singularistic standpoint of his *Structure of Social Actions* with its "unit act" and its voluntaristic "means-end schema." This standpoint and schema are now practically abandoned in favor of a more "generalized" level of analysis (SS9), and the Weberian seminominalistic and singularistic framework of actions, actors and roles is replaced by a more adequate "realistic" framework of social system, cultural systems, and personality system or by the "whole play," of which roles, actions, and actors are but components.[59]

Substantively, Parsons' theories of society were worked out by way of a conception of pattern variables conceived as dimensions of the social system which was, in turn, conceived to be the primary social reality. Personality, society, and culture were conceived as independent boundary-maintaining systems. Finally, the social system was conceived as a set of forces in equilibrium, divided into component subsystems. The great subsystems of society were conceived as receiving influences from one or more of four sources (physical nature, the biological organism, personality, and culture) and, like a great factory, processing these influences into some sort of output. The integrating summary of his conception of the social system was presented by Parsons in one of his contributions to *Theories of Society* in 1961.

The presuppositions of his functionalistic theory are compactly summarized by Parsons in the Max Black symposium. Parsons maintains that an action system is constituted by the internalization in personality and the organism and the institutionalization in society and culture of patterns of meaning. Patterns of meaning comprise feelings, values, and ideas. The goals of the units of the action system (that is, of the people who act) must, Parsons insists, represent contributions to the functioning of the whole. To the extent that an action system becomes differentiated, a balance must be struck between definiteness in the relationships between the units and flexibility with regard both to the system and to extra-system factors. Such a balance (between the needs of individuals and the needs of society) is achieved by the institutionalization of generalized normative patterns compatible with the varied requirements of special situations. Such an action system, moreover, is subdivided into four functional subsystems between which direct interchanges may occur.[60]

At the time of his formulations in *Theories of Society* and his summary statement for the Black symposium on his theories, Parsons' functionalism was virtually complete. His activities since have consisted largely in working out the details and planing down the rough spots in the conception of society as a system within which all subparts operate interdependently to realize the values of the whole. In the newspaper report on Parsons' retirement, Robert Reinhold called attention to the biological analogies in terms of which Parsons had ordered his conception of society.

> Like biological systems, he argues, social systems have regulatory mechanisms that allow them to return to equilibrium after each disturbance. Thus, while many conflicting forces are crossing through the body of the system, the mechanisms of social control tend to keep the system as a whole in dynamic equilibrium.
>
> One of the main cornerstones of Parsonian theory is what he calls the "four-function paradigm." According to this concept, a social system's structure is governed by the way it meets four basic needs. The system differentiates into subsystems that serve to satisfy these needs.
>
> The four are: "goal attainment," or the methods by which the system mobilizes to achieve its goals: "adaptation," or adjustment to the environment for survival and to acquire facilities, such as capital, to reach the goals; "integration," the internal relations of the units of the system to each other, designed to reconcile conflicts and maintain cohesion; and "pattern maintenance," the means by which the actors deal with pressures to deviate from accepted norms.[61]

C. Wright Mills: Phase III (1958–1962)

Some persons, even some close to Mills, are already visualizing phase II of Mills' intellectual development as his greatest period. One estimate of *The New Men of Power, White Collar,* and *The Power Elite* runs as follows:

> These books were sociology in the classic sense of "the study of society" rather than the new, compressed, and jargon-ridden styles of the profession which Mills so brilliantly analyzed but dismissed in *The Sociological Imagination.* . . . But in the last few years Mills was doing something

further, in short, books that he did not present as sociology but which nevertheless were attacked for not being sociology. He thought of these books, *The Causes of World War Three* and *Listen Yankee*, as a high order of "pamphleteering" which frankly included exhortation as well as analysis.[62]

Perhaps in the long run it may be true that phase II of Mills' work will be viewed as his most important period. If so, he will drop to comparatively minor significance in the total picture of the development of sociological theory. On the other hand, there is little question that the work in his third phase was most original. However, how the work of Mills' third phase will eventually be evaluated does not depend on him alone, but on what happens to the tradition which does or does not flow from it.

The effect of a man's place in the tradition on the evaluation of a theorist may be clarified by two examples. E. A. Ross wrote brilliant semiclassical studies (his *Social Psychology* and his *Social Control*) while adhering to a branch of social behaviorism. He then shifted his forces to a branch of sociological formalism, which later died out. In the evaluation of Ross' work by later thinkers, there is a tendency simply to dismiss that large part of a lifetime of work. Alfred Vierkandt displays a different fate. After brilliant contributions to positivistic organicism, Vierkandt shifted the main impetus of his work of phenomenological sociology which he pioneered. Late developments in phenomenological sociology are still under way. While Ross has some of the properties of a man who missed his deepest calling, Vierkandt does not.

In the third phase of his work Mills achieved a kind of fulfillment of the impetus already discernible to those of us who knew him as a graduate student toward bringing his reformist and theoretical inclinations together into a single formulation. Moreover, there seems to be no justification whatsoever for separating Mills' formulations in his article for the Llewellyn Gross *Symposium*, in *Images of Man*, and in *The Sociological Imagination* from the formulations of *The Causes of World War Three*, *Listen Yankee*, and *The Marxists*. The latter group of works are applications of the position theoretically argued in the former. These works belong together as a single unified point of view.

In the Gross *Symposium* Mills announced his radical break with empiricism.

> Now I do not like to do empirical work if I can possibly avoid it. It means a great deal of trouble if one has no staff, and, if one does employ a staff,

then the staff is often more trouble than the work itself. . . . In our situation, empirical work as such is for beginning students and for those who aren't able to handle the complexities of big problems; it is also for highly formal men who do not care what they study so long as it appears to be orderly.[63]

One could not have a more forthright break with the pragmatism and social behaviorism of Mills' early period than this. His one-time idols, Pierce and Weber, whose empiricism was deeply entrenched, must have turned over in their graves at such an utterance.

Later the same year, Mills generalized his anti-empiricism into an attack on science itself.

> The cultural meaning of physical science . . . is becoming doubtful. . . . The obvious conquest of nature . . . is felt by men of the over-developed societies to be virtually complete. And now in these societies, science— the chief instrument of this conquest—is felt to be foot-loose, aimless, and in need of reappraisal. . . . Many cultural workmen have come to feel that "science is a false and pretentious Messiah."[64]

The break with the pragmatists and social behaviorists was growing more trenchant. It assumed a most direct form in his passionate rejection of the individualism of one of his youthful idols, Max Weber.

> In the more political essays of Max Weber, I am inclined to believe the classic tradition in sociological thinking comes to a moral climax, a crisis of orientation, which we have by no means overcome. In fact, we have not even confronted it squarely. Weber presents the social world as a chaos of values, a hopeless plurality of gods; his is the pessimistic world of a classic liberal of supreme intelligence and enormous knowledge, thinking at the end of the liberal era and finding no basis for decision, no criterion other than his own personal will and integrity.[65]

No conservative has ever rejected individuality as a principle with greater violence! In the same context Mills welcomes all evidence of support of his own growing antirationalism—another aspect of his youthful theoretical orientation which he was in process of rejecting.

> Karl Mannheim's essay on rationality contains the seeds of the most profound criticism of the secular rationalism of Western civilization. He did not work it out in just this way, but the passage given here is among the best writings of a man who is, I believe, one of the two or three most vital and important sociologists of the inter-war period.[66]

With the rejection of empiricism, science, individualism, and finally, rationalism, Mills' departure from the ranks of the social behaviorists is complete and irreversible. His violent attack on the branches of current sociology as he defines them flows from his identification of them as empirical, scientific, individualistic, or rationalistic, as the case may be. A single sentence in *Images of Man* sums up the foundation of his opposition: "The moral crisis of this humanist tradition, reflected in sociology, coincides with the retreat of our generation of social scientists into 'mere fact.' "[67]

However, the rejection of individualism, science, empiricism, and rationalism did not exhaust Mills' message in the period of 1959–1962. He also outlined his positive views of the intellectual tradition and society. At the same time that he rejected scientific sociology ("all sociology worthy of the name is 'historical sociology.' ")[68] and denied in principle its capacity to make lawlike generalizations of a scientific type,[69] he made claims of an extremity almost unparalleled since August Comte for sociology as the intellectual synthesis of modern man.

> I am going to contend that journalists and scholars, artists and publics, scientists and editors, are coming to expect . . . the sociological imagination. . . . The social sciences are becoming the common denominator of our cultural period, and the sociological imagination our most needed quality of mind.[70]

Since sociology has been denied a scientific character, it can only have—for Mills—a moral and ethical character. Mills leaves no doubt as to his view of the proper task of sociology.

> As social scientists, we located ourselves. . . . It is . . . the political task of the social scientist . . . to address his work to the other three types of men I have classified in terms of power and knowledge. . . . To those with power and with awareness of it, he imputes . . . responsibility for such structural consequences as he finds . . . influenced by their decisions and their lack of decisions. . . . To those whose actions have such consequences, but who do not seem aware of them, he directs whatever he has found out about those consequences. He attempts to educate and then, again, he imputes responsibility. To those . . . regularly without power and whose awareness is confined to their everyday *milieux*, he . . . states what he has found out concerning the actions of the more powerful.[71]

In short, the task of sociology is to supply the moral guidance required by the times.

It is difficult to see how *The Causes of World War Three* and *Listen Yankee* can be described as something other than sociology for Mills.

To be sure, they are propaganda. But that is precisely what Mills maintains *true* sociology to be. *The Causes of World War Three* is a shrill call for action.

> The withdrawal of cultural workmen from politics, in America especially, is part of the international default, which is both cultural and political, of the Western world today. The young complacents of America, the tired old fighters, the smug liberals, the shrill ladies of jingoist culture—they are all quite free. Nobody looks them up. Nobody has to. ... They do not examine the U.S.A. as an over-developed society full of ugly waste and the deadening of human responsibility, honoring ignorance and the cheerful robot, pronouncing the barren doctrine and submitting gladly, even with eagerness, to the uneasy fun of a leisureless and emptying existence.[72]

Listen Yankee contains interesting proposals, such as:

> The U.S. Government should at once and unilaterally cease all further production of "extermination" weapons—all A- and B- bombs and nuclear warheads included. It should announce the size of its present stockpile, along with a schedule for reducing it or converting it, so far as is technically possible, to devices for peacetime uses.[73]

Mills' proposals take so little account of the organization of nation-states as to amount to empty rhetoric which, at best, offers some comfort to the Soviet bloc of nations.

However, it is in *Listen Yankee* that Mills' positive views of society in his period of fulfillment are most fully expressed. *Listen Yankee* is not about "what is really happening in Cuba" at all; it is too filled with inadequate, partial, and even false information for that. Nor is *Listen Yankee* the voice of the Cuban revolutionary which C. Wright Mills only reports. Mills' hypothetical Cuban revolutionary expresses too many judgments which no Cuban revolutionary ever thought, judgments which could only have been furnished by Mills himself.

The hypothetical Cuban revolutionary in *Listen Yankee* is a vehicle permitting Mills, for once, to speak positively out of his own dreams. Mills is not the first outstanding man who spoke most directly and forcefully for himself only in those moments when he presented himself as the mouthpiece, or interpreter, or reporter, or the prophet of his god. Among nineteenth-century thinkers one is reminded of Kierkegaard, who spoke most fully for himself through various pseudonyms, each of which permitted the expression in relatively pure form of some aspect of his highly ambivalent nature. Or again, Nietzsche spoke most powerfully for himself as Zarathustra.

Listen Yankee is no very significant or authentic account of the revolution in Cuba. Its hero is the mouthpiece, not of the Cuban revolutionary, but of Mills. *Listen Yankee* is essentially a religious-morality tale manufactured out of some events and fragments of items drawn from recent Cuban experience. Its religious-morality character is shown by the blackness of its agents of darkness. (U.S. capitalists and the American State Department ready to sustain the pressure of innocent Cuban peasant girls into prostitution as a by-product of their imperialistic plans) and the unstained goodness of its agents of light (Castro and the revolutionaries). The limited potential of Cuba for industrialization is thrust aside, the pressure of its population on its resources is ignored. Cuba is visualized as a potentially self-sufficient land of plenty. This plentitude is to be achieved by such devices as a happy, productive chicken coop in every yard. To criticize this as impractical, however, would be to miss the essentially utopian character of the society which Mills visualizes the Cubans as creating.

One of the most striking of all properties of *Listen Yankee* is the emergence of Fidel Castro as an apotheosized superman, as a living savior, a god on earth. No slightest hint of criticism ever attaches to his figure or actions in Mills' account.

> Fidel Castro . . . promotes not the cult of the individual but the facts of the revolution. . . . He is the most directly radical and democratic force in Cuba. . . . Before any problem is solved, Fidel spends long hours on the TV. . . . He explains and he educates, and after he speaks almost every doubt has gone away. Never before has such a force of public opinion prevailed for so long and so intimately with power. . . . His speeches actually create the revolutionary consciousness—and the work gets done. It is fantastic to see how, as it goes along, the revolutionary process transforms one layer after another of the population. And always there is Fidel's anti-bureaucratic personality.[74]

The touching spectacle emerges of a Columbia professor, one of the oustanding contemporary sociologists, an author of world renown, an ever-so-ready critic of everyone else, subordinating himself to the authoritarian figure of a Cuban revolutionary leader. Surely the atmosphere is religious, and the spirit medieval. The high point of Mills' expression of those sentiments is appropriately contained in a chapter entitled "Revolutionary Euphoria," and surely no better description could be made of his mood than his own.

> Everyone has day dreams, but for most people these dreams are never related to their everyday life. By our revolution, we Cubans have made

The Big Connection, between fantasy and reality, and now we are living
in it. To us to live in this connection, that is the fact of our revolution.[75]

Formulations such as these which appear over and over again in
his last works show that Mills had found his own fulfillment. The final
position achieved by him thus can be seen as a form of left-wing
humanistic collectivism. Mills was quite correct in objecting to the
designation of his position as Marxist—for in contrast to the Marxists
he has rejected science and the fusion of left-wing collectivism and
science, which are peculiar to Marxism and all other forms of scientific socialism.

Even stylistically the last phase of Mills' work has the properties of
a fulfillment. One of the clearest signs of the collectivist is that he is
most at home when he deals with mass themes for which a generic,
slogan-like style is most appropriate. On the other hand, the true
collectivist is least sure of himself when he deals with individuals and
the problems of personal psychology. The reverse is true of the person who by temperament and training is individualistic—masses always seem like empty categories and the language appropriate to
them is made up of shibboleths which defy rational analysis.

Mills' temperamental collectivism (appearing in the inverse form
of a strident, anti-authoritarianism in his early period and as the
surprising subordination to Fidel Castro as an authoritarian symbol
in *Listen Yankee*) is manifest in the inadequacy (notable in a mind
so brilliant) with which he handles all issues of individual psychology.
A striking incapacity to take the role of the other is manifest throughout *White Collar*, for example, where negative characterizations are
assembled for one group after another. Particularly significant along
the same lines is the almost complete lack of understanding of the
psychology of women. From his earliest writings to his last, women
appear in Mills' writing either as the most innocent and pure angels,
defenseless and subject to cynical commercial exploitation, or they
appear as the most hardened tramps. The subtle richness of feminine
psychology finds no place in Mills' writings. He is most at home when
individuals are reduced to categories. It is from this point that Mills'
reduction of the problem of motivation to strategies of deceit must
be viewed. He did not understand individuals, and in the end cast out
individuality as a chaotic principle.

Similarly, Mills' style approaches its most characteristic form in his
later works. Despite its vigor, his style is not stripped down and terse.
There is a kind of oratorical excess about it. Mills does not draw out
his analyses, nor systematically explore themes so much as to make
an assault upon them. A sort of oratorical build-up is followed by the

firing off of volleys of sloganlike phrases. In his latest works, these phrases assume a stereotyped form and the number of capitalized words increases. It is as if a tense, strident mood expressed itself naturally in upper case letters.

However, explorations such as these must be left to Mills' biographer. Here such style notes are only tentatively taken as possible further evidence that the last phase of Mills' work was not a deviation, as has been suggested, but a fulfillment.

Final Notes on Mills and Parsons

Talcott Parsons, Mills' foremost opponent on the current American scene, also began his career as a social behaviorist. There were, to be sure, differences. Parsons was partly influenced by Marshall in a manner not true for Mills. Mills was influenced by Veblen to a degree that seems to find no counterpart in Parsons. However, they share an influence by Weber.

It may be possible that their common social behaviorism was a product of a combination of their middle-class derivation, the intellectual *milieu,* and the Great Depression which had seriously shaken men's faith in the infallibility of the collective, while in America, at least, not replacing it with a new faith in left-wing collectivism. Whatever the cause, since World War II both Parsons and Mills have been in evolution toward collectivistic positions. Parsons has moved to right-wing collectivism and scientism, which has placed him in the stout position of defender of the *status quo.* By contrast, Mills has been in evolution toward a left-wing collectivism, but without the old optimist faith in scientific progress of Marxism and scientific socialism. Ironically, in their orientation to science Parsons and Mills have exchanged positions. Parsons opened his career with a forthright attack on positivism (the scientific tradition in social science), but as his functionalism neared perfection he quietly re-introduced positivistic orientations in strengthened form. Mills opened his career with an almost doctrinaire adherence to the logical positivism and scientism of Charles Pierce, and closed it with violent attacks upon science as "a false and pretentious Messiah, or at least a highly ambiguous element in modern civilization."[76]

In the 1960s events have been moving beyond the redoubtable warriors of the fifties. C. Wright Mills was cut down by an untimely death. Even before this, developments in Cuba, including Castro's identification with Russian Communism, had betrayed the accuracy of Mills' interpretations. If Harvey Swados, Mills' most intimate friend, reported correctly, Mills' response to these developments betrays the essentially religious character of *Listen Yankee*. He maintains that Mills at the end:

> ... was torn between defending *Listen Yankee*, as a good and honest book, and acknowledging publicly for the first time in his life that he had been terribly wrong. ... The tension was too much, the decline of the revolution, atop his personal pains, was too much. I can only add that he declared to me in his last weeks that he was becoming more and more impressed with the psychological and intellectual relevance of nonviolent resistance and absolute pacifism.[77]

With rather horrifying speed Castro turned out to be Mills' "god that failed." Swados seems to suspect that this was a component in Mills' last fatal heart attack.

The fate of an in-group politician rarely displays the same pathos as that of a rebel guerrilla and leader of an unorthodox transient sect. He may, as has Parsons, acquire a considerable estate in the profession which he is able to administer gracefully if only he assumes the role of elder statesman at long last above the conflicts of the hour. That Parsons seems inclined to assume this role appears in the closing pages of self-defense against his critics of the Black symposium.

> To me, what I call the theory of action was, in its core—which I take to be the social system in its relation to the personality of the individual—founded in the generation of Durkheim, Weber, and Freud, with of course a very complex set of other influences, a few of which have been mentioned here. With the very perceptible fading of the influence of the older economic individualism—in its scientific rather than political reference—and the older personality-individualism, it is a striking fact that *general* orientations in this field have, in recent years, tended increasingly to polarize between a non-dogmatic and non-political "Marxian" position and one which in the broadest sense may be called one or another version of the theory of action. The most important exception to this is probably the influence of the "culture and personality" school which is an attempted direct *fusion* of the atomistic and idealistic trends, as distinguished from what I have symbolized as a "marriage."[78]

One must never forget that what Parsons (and earlier, Shils) calls the "theory of action" is his name for functionalism. It is a form of wholism or collectivism which has little to do with the social action theory of Max Weber which is an individualistic (or atomistic) form of social behaviorism.

This statement by Parsons, made in 1961, amounts to an admission that Parsons' theory is not the sole legitimate heir of sociology after all, for neo-Marxian conflict theory is undergoing a revival and becoming an increasingly important rival of functionalism. Moreover, the same statement admits that all individualistic (or atomistic) positions are not as antiquated as was once assumed. Parsons has been correct. As the 1960s have unfolded, the number of attacks upon functionalism have increased. Forms of neo-Marxian conflict theory have continued to develop. Moreover, all forms of social behaviorism have shown unexpected vitality.

Even Parsons' position in the profession has been subjected to what amounts to symbolic assault and transformation. In 1963 some persons, outraged at the failure of the nominating committee of the American Sociological Association to place Parsons' old rival at Harvard, Pitirim Sorokin, on the ballot for the presidency, threatened a write-in campaign. As pressure built up, the nominating committee was forced to reissue a new slate of candidates including Sorokin. The society responded by electing Sorokin the next president of the Association.

It would be a mistake to view Sorokin's election to the presidency of the American Sociological Association as a "rejection" of Talcott Parsons. It would be as misleading to draw the conclusion that Parsons is being rejected as to interpret the numerous tributes and memorial volumes to C. Wright Mills as a posthumous attempt by professional sociologists to join Mills' peculiar form of antiscientific sectarianism. The insistence upon the part of the professional society of extending to Parsons' old rival the highest honor it is able to bestow amounted to acknowledging him to be an elder of equal honor. It implied that in the minds of many, Parsons was now but one of the elders. And the tributes and memorials to C. Wright Mills amount to the claim by the profession to the remains of one of its own prodigal sons.

The 1970s may develop new proponents to represent the great divisions, but Parsons and Mills will remain the titans of the 1950s and 1960s as sociology's heroes who, at the mid-twentieth century, epitomized better than most men in their theories and their careers the contrast and tension between the scientific and humanistic wings of contemporary American sociology.

Notes

1. Don Martindale, "Talcott Parsons' Theoretical Metamorphosis from Social Behaviorism to Macrofunctionalism," *The Alpha Kappa Deltan*, XXIX, no. 1 (Winter 1959): 38–46.

2. See Edward C. Devereux, Jr., "Parsons' Sociological Theory," in *The Social Theories of Talcott Parsons*, ed. Max Black (Englewood Cliffs, N.J.: Prentice-Hall, 1961), p. 6.

3. Talcott Parsons, "A Short Account of My Intellectual Development," *Alpha Kappa Deltan* (Winter 1959), p. 3.

4. Ibid., p. 4.

5. Hans Gerth, mimeographed statement read at a Memorial Meeting, Columbia University, April 16, 1962, p. 3.

6. Pitirim Sorokin, *A Long Journey* (New Haven, Conn.: College and University Press, 1963), pp. 243–44.

7. Devereux, "Parsons' Sociological Theory," in *The Social Theories of Talcott Parsons*, ed. Black, p. 4.

8. Sorokin, *A Long Journey*, p. 251.

9. Irving Louis Horowitz, ed., *Power, Politics, and People* (New York: Oxford University Press, 1963), pp. 6–7.

10. Devereux, "Parson's Sociological Theory," in *The Social Theories of Talcott Parsons*, ed. Black, p. 6.

11. Sorokin, *A Long Journey*, p. 251.

12. Dan Wakefield, "Taking It Big: A Memoir of C. Wright Mills," *Atlantic*, September 1961, p. 66.

13. Ibid., p. 68.

14. Harvey Swados, "C. Wright Mills: A Personal Memoir," *Dissent* (Winter 1963), p. 37.

15. Ibid., p. 40.

16. Saul Landau, "C. Wright Mills—The Last Six Months," *Root and Branch* (Berkeley, Calif., Spring 1963), pp. 7–8.

17. Swados, "Mills: A Personal Memoir," p. 38.

18. Landau, "Mills—The Last Six Months," p. 14.

19. Talcott Parsons, "Comment on Llewelyn Gross' Preface to a Metatheoretical Framework for Sociology," *The American Journal of Sociology*, LXVII, no. 2 (September 1961): 138.

20. Swados, "Mills: A Personal Memoir," p. 41.

21. Robert Reinhold, "A Mentor of Sociologists Retires After 42 Years at Harvard Post," *New York Times*, 14 June 1973. Reproduced in *ASA Footnotes*, August 1973, p. 3.

22. Ibid.

23. Swados, "Mills: A Personal Memoir," p. 35. As a young parent, Swados observed, Mills was completely indifferent to his infant offspring, observing that at this stage they were without personality and not worth bothering with until a few years later.

24. Talcott Parsons, *The Social System* (Glencoe: The Free Press, 1951), p. 12.

25. C. Wright Mills, *White Collar* (New York: Oxford University Press, 1953), p. 132.

26. Wakefield, "Taking It Big," p. 65.

27. Mills, *White Collar*, p. 133. Italics mine.

28. Mills, *The Power Elite* (New York: Oxford University Press, 1956), p. 72. Italics mine.

29. Ibid., p. 82.

30. Ibid., p. 83.

31. Ibid., p. 82.

32. Edward Shils, "The Calling of Sociology," *Theories of Society,* edited by Talcott Parsons, Edward Shils, Kaspar D. Naegele, and Jesse R. Pitts (New York: The Free Press of Glencoe, 1961), vol. 2, p. 1410.

33. Ibid., p. 1413.

34. Ibid., p. 1420.

35. Ibid., p. 1422.

36. Ibid.

37. Talcott Parsons in Black, ed., *Social Theories of Talcott Parsons,* pp. 362–63.

38. C. Wright Mills, *Images of Man* (New York: George Braziller, 1960), pp. 4–5.

39. Ibid., p. 11.

40. Ibid., p. 12.

41. C. Wright Mills, *The Marxists* (New York: Dell, 1962), p. 13.

42. Ibid., p. 16.

43. Ibid., pp. 13–14.

44. Reinhold, *ASA Footnotes,* p. 3.

45. Mills, *The Sociological Imagination* (New York: Oxford University Press, 1959), p. 49.

46. Ibid., p. 32.

47. Ibid., p. 53.

48. Ibid., p. 95.

49. Parsons, "A Short Account," p. 4.

50. Talcott Parsons, *The Structure of Social Action* (New York: McGraw-Hill, 1937).

51. Ibid. p. 740.

52. Hans H. Gerth and C. Wright Mills, *Character and Social Structure* (New York: Harcourt, Brace, 1953), p. 114.

53. Ibid., p. 116.

54. Ibid., p. 117.

55. Ibid., p. 122.

56. Ibid., p. 127.

57. Pitirim A. Sorokin, "Similarities and Dissimilarities between Two Sociological Systems," mimeographed, Notes on T. Parsons and E. A. Shils, eds., *Toward a General Theory of Action* (Cambridge: Harvard University Press, 1951), and T. Parsons, *The Social System* (Glencoe, Ill.: The Free Press, 1951), p. 1.

58. Ibid., pp. 9–10.

59. Pitirim A. Sorokin, *Sociological Theories of Today* (New York: Harper & Row, 1966), pp. 431–32. In this volume Sorokin extended the comparison between his own and Parsons' theories in the mimeographed paper widely circulated throughout the society several years earlier. Also see Parsons' own formulation in the Black symposium, p. 360.

60. Talcott Parsons, in Black, ed., *Social Theories of Talcott Parsons.* This is a summary of Parsons' argument appearing between pp. 342–44.

61. Reinhold, *ASA Footnotes,* p. 3.

62. Dan Wakefield, "C. Wright Mills," *The Nation,* 14 April 1962, p. 331.

63. C. Wright Mills, "On Intellectual Craftsmanship," *Symposium on Sociological Theory,* ed. Llewellyn Gross (Evanston, Ill.: Row, Peterson, 1949), p. 35.

64. Mills, *The Sociological Imagination,* pp. 15–16.

65. Mills, *Images of Man,* p. 7.

66. Ibid., p. 12.

67. Ibid., p. 7.

68. *The Sociological Imagination,* p. 146.

69. Ibid., pp. 149–50.

70. Ibid., pp. 5–13.

71. Ibid., p. 185.

72. C. Wright Mills, *The Causes of World War Three* (New York: Simon & Schuster, 1958), p. 127.

73. C. Wright Mills, *Listen Yankee* (New York: McGraw-Hill, 1960), pp. 122–23.

74. Ibid.

75. Ibid., p. 113.

76. *Sociological Imagination,* p. 14.

77. Swados, "Mills: A Personal Memoir," p. 42.

78. Black, ed., *Social Theories of Talcott Parsons,* pp. 361–62.

Selected Bibliography

C. Wright Mills

The Causes of World War Three. New York: Simon & Schuster, 1958.

Character and Social Structure (with Hans H. Gerth). New York: Harcourt, Brace, 1953.

Listen Yankee: The Revolution in Cuba. New York: McGraw-Hill, 1960.

The New Men of Power: America's Labor Leaders. New York: Harcourt, Brace, 1948.

The Power Elite. New York: Oxford University Press, 1956.

Power, Politics, and People: The Collected Essays of C. Wright Mills. New York: Oxford University Press, 1963.

The Puerto Rican Journey: New York's New Migrants, with Clarence Senior and Rose K. Goldsen. New York: Oxford University Press, 1950.

The Sociological Imagination. New York: Oxford University Press, 1959.

White Collar: The American Middle Classes. New York: Oxford University Press, 1953.

Talcott Parsons

American Sociology, ed. Talcott Parsons. New York: Basic Books, 1968.

Economy and Society, with Neil J. Smelser. Glencoe, Ill.: The Free Press, 1956.

Essays in Sociological Theory Pure and Applied. Glencoe, Ill.: The Free Press, 1949.

Essays in Sociological Theory, rev. ed. Glencoe, Ill.: The Free Press, 1954, 1967.

Family, Socialization, and Interaction Process, with Robert F. Bales, James

Olds, Morris Zelditch, and Philip E. Slater. Glencoe, Ill.: The Free Press, 1955.

Politics and Social Structure. New York: The Free Press, 1969.

Social Structure and Personality. New York: The Free Press, 1964.

The Social System. Glencoe, Ill.: The Free Press, 1951.

Societies: Evolutionary and Comparative Perspectives. Englewood Cliffs, N.J.: Prentice-Hall, 1966.

Sociological Theory and Modern Society. New York: The Free Press, 1967.

Structure and Process in Modern Societies. Glencoe, Ill.: The Free Press, 1960.

The Structure of Social Action. New York: McGraw-Hill, 1937.

Theories of Society, co-editor with Edward Shils, Kaspar D. Naegele, and Jesse R. Pitts, 2 vols. New York: The Free Press, 1961.

Toward a General Theory of Action, with Edward A. Shils. Cambridge: Harvard University Press, 1951, 1962.

Working Papers in the Theory of Action, with Robert F. Bales and Edward A. Shils. Glencoe, Ill.: The Free Press, 1953.

4

Pitirim A. Sorokin:
Soldier of Fortune

Pitirim A. Sorokin's bibliography as of January, 1963, consisted of thirty-five books (some of them multivolume works) and more than four hundred articles, essays, editorials, and papers published in scientific journals of various countries. A large number of Sorokin's books have been translated into other languages: *Contemporary Sociological Theories* has been translated from English into eleven of the major languages of mankind; *The Crisis of Our Age* into eight; other volumes into a lesser number of languages. By 1963, forty-two translations of Sorokin's published volumes had been completed. Other translations were in preparation, and Sorokin was composing other books.

In terms of comparative productivity and numbers of translations, no other sociologist equals Sorokin. Talcott Parsons, who is held by numerous contemporary scholars to be the foremost sociologist in America, had, as of 1960, a bibliography of ten books (which included two translations, jointly edited volumes, and re-published volumes of essays). Parsons had at this time also a total of eighty-two published articles. Little of Parsons' work had been translated into other languages at the time. C. Wright Mills, who is sometimes claimed to be the most important sociologist of America's post-World War II period, had a total productivity of eleven volumes (which included one joint translation, two co-authored volumes, an edited anthology, and a book of essays published posthumously). A bibliography including every essay, review, book note, and comment compiled by Mills' disciple still brought Mills' published bibliography to only 205 items.[1] A total of eighteen translations had been made of Mills' works at that time. Sorokin's productivity in books, in articles, and in the number of translations greatly outdistanced that of Talcott Parsons and C. Wright Mills, for each of whom greater significance often has been claimed. Sorokin—so far as this can be checked—seems to have been the most productive and most translated sociologist who ever lived.

Sorokin was founder, first professor, and then chairman of the department of sociology at the University of St. Petersburg (Leningrad). He published five volumes in law and sociology between 1920 and 1922. After his final arrest and banishment by the Soviet government, he became professor of sociology at the University of Minnesota. During his occupancy of this position (1924–1930), he published five major works. He left Minnesota to become founder of the department of sociology and the first chairman at Harvard University. In 1948 he established the Harvard Research Center in Creative Altruism, of which he remained director until his retirement from Harvard.

During a long productive career Sorokin played a major role in founding a number of sociological areas such as the sociology of revolution, the sociology of mobility and stratification, the sociology of calamity, and the sociology of cultural morphology. He had a role in the careers of a number of major contemporary sociologists who worked with him as graduate students or came within his sphere of influence. In his autobiography Sorokin offered the following list of contemporary sociologists influenced by him.

When, in January, 1962, Charles and Zona Loomis' *Modern Social Theories* was published, in my letter to the authors I observed that practically all the sociologists whose theories are examined in the volume (Kingsley Davis, G. C. Homans, R. K. Merton, T. Parsons, R. Williams, and including Professor Loomis himself and W. E. Moore, the editor of the Van Nostrand series in sociology) were either graduate students or an instructor (T. Parsons), or an associate (G. Homans), or a visiting lecturer (H. Becker) in the department during my chairmanship. To these names of the leading American sociologists I can add several others, such as Professors C. A. Anderson, R. F. Bales, B. Barber, W. Bash, R. Bauer, C. Q. Berger, R. Bierstedt, G. Blackwell, R. Chamblis, A. Davis, N. Demerath, N. DeNood, J. Donovan, R. DuWors, J. B. Ford, R. Hanson, D. Hatch, H. Hitt, L. Haak, J. Fichter, W. Firey, H. Johnston, F. Kluckhohn,

J. B. Knox, M. Levy, V. Parenton, A. Pierce, B. Reed, J. and M. Riley, E. Schuler, T. Lynn Smith, C. Tilly, E. A. Tiryakian, N. Whetten, Logan Wilson, and others who did their graduate work in the department during my chairmanship.[2]

And yet Sorokin never became the center of a school or founded a movement.

Fortunately, Sorokin has left an unusually full record of the events of his personal life, including *Leaves from a Russian Diary, A Long Journey,* and the autobiographical introduction to *Pitirim A. Sorokin in Review.*

The Major Events of Sorokin's Life

Few sociologists living today can boast of lives of such variety as Sorokin whose destiny took him from the frontier of northern Russia through the stormy events of the Russian Revolution to the position of the world's most eminent sociologist in the 1960s.

Sorokin was one of three boys born to an Urgo-Finnish peasant girl and an itinerant artisan Russian father. He was born in the northern Russian Province of Vologda among the Komi people on January 21, 1889. His mother died when he was three years old. The Komi were peasants who supplemented their subsistence agriculture by hunting, trapping, lumbering, and fishing. They lived in village communities with a clergyman teacher, medical practitioner, policeman, mayor, and clerk. Their agrarian communities were self-governing like the German *Gemeinschaften* and Russian *mir* and *obschina.* Land was held in common by the villagers and periodically redistributed among individual families as their conditions changed. The elective authorities were charged with such tasks as the building of schools, medical centers, and the housing for cultural activities. Though many beliefs, legends, and rituals persisted from their pre-Christian pagan past, the Komi were Russian Orthodox. Families were close-knit, serving as a mutual welfare institution with their obligations of mutual aid to family members.

At the time of the death of Sorokin's mother, his younger brother went to live with a maternal aunt. Sorokin and his elder brother remained with their father, assisting him in his work as an itinerant craftsman. Wherever the father received assignments, the boys were temporarily placed in school. Also, from time to time during his childhood years Sorokin periodically vacationed or found temporary refuge with his mother's people.

Sorokin's father was born in the ancient city of Veliki Ustyug, where he became a master craftsman in gold, silver, and iron ornamental work. Sorokin and his brother accompanied him as he moved from village to village in search of assignments. Sorokin reported that his father had the reputation for being a reliable, honest, and comparatively skillful workman. However, as the years went by periods of sobriety were punctuated by excessive drinking that at times resulted in delirium tremens. After one unusually violent period which led to attacks on the boys (Sorokin was eleven at the time, his brother fourteen) they set out as independent itinerant artisans. For two years Sorokin's elder brother guided their mutual affairs, securing sufficient commissions to survive. Sorokin's brother continued to seek an education, and the two separated when Sorokin won a scholarship to a "normal" school. He did so well there as to win encouragement and support for entrance into a seminary.

Both of Sorokin's brothers eventually became involved in the Russian Revolution. The elder brother continued to practice the trade of an itinerant craftsman for a time, then moved to St. Petersburg, working as a craftsman, salesman, and clerk. In 1918 he was arrested by the communists for antirevolutionary activities and executed. Sorokin's younger brother remained with a maternal aunt until he was drafted into the Russian army and was stationed in a Russian city. Until termination of his military service, this brother remained in the city, becoming successively a bookkeeper, clerk, and salesman. He married and raised two children. He was arrested with little justification, Sorokin believed, for subversive activities and was sent to prison, where he died.

Sorokin's itinerant life with his father and elder brother made formal schooling a hit-and-miss affair. However, he was systematically enrolled in various village schools in which his father and brother secured commissions. Moreover, since the work of the itinerant artisan was usually secured from the priest or some other member of the village intelligentsia, Sorokin came into contact with the highest cultural and intellectual traditions of the region. Moreover, travel from place to place supplied a wide base of comparative experience. Sorokin stated that he often received encouragement in his studies and the loan of books from teachers, clergymen, and more enlightened peasants with whom he came in contact.

When an advanced grade school was opened in Gam village, where Sorokin and his elder brother were working, Sorokin volunteered for the entrance examinations, which he passed with flying colors. He was awarded a scholarship of five rubles ($2.50) which paid his room and board for an entire year! The scholarship was renewed for each of the three years of the school curriculum.

At this time in Russia one of the few avenues to higher circles open to bright peasant and artisan youths was through the church. Sorokin's peasant relatives were pious Russian Orthodox in religion. Moreover, his travels with his father and brother took him primarily to the village churches for commissions. The church emerged as the single most glamorous institution of Sorokin's childhood. The village priests, for their part, often took an interest in the avid motherless youth, loaning him books and encouraging his reading. Sorokin remembered much reading in an old quarto volume of the lives of the saints which impressed him as an ideal outlet for his own abilities. He became a lay preacher at neighborhood gatherings of peasants on long winter evenings.

> If there are elements of mysticism in my theories, as several scholars assert, such mystic and tragic strains were set therein at an early age by the tragic mysteries of the Mass and by the trying experiences of my life.[3]

The spell of a clerical career and his success in the schools of his native province led Sorokin to ascend the primary route up and out of his peasant-artisan background. When in 1903, at the age of fourteen, he graduated from the Gam school, he won a scholarship for the Khrenovo Teachers Seminary in Kostroma Province. The Seminary was a denominational school under the jurisdiction of the Holy Synod of the Russian Orthodox Church. It trained teachers for the Synod's elementary schools.

In 1904, under the impact of the Russo-Japanese War, and in 1905, under the influence of the Revolution, the theological seminaries were shaken by the winds of doctrine. Within two years after his move to the Seminary, Sorokin reported that his previous religiosity had been replaced by a "semi-atheistic rejection of the theologies and rituals of the Russian Orthodox Church."[4]

Under the influence of the new revolutionary ferment, Sorokin became a member of the Social Revolutionary Party. At schools and in nearby villages he preached the Social Revolutionary gospel, as earlier he had preached religious orthodoxy to pious peasants. He was arrested and thrown into jail by the czarist police, but was—as was usual for political prisoners at the time—well treated. In jail he came in contact with the intoxicating excitement of the political prisoners and intellectuals. "Daily discussions and an intensive reading of the works of Mikhailovsky, Lavrov, Marx, Engels, Bakunin, Kropotkin, Tolstoi, Plenkhanov, Tehernoff, Lenin, and other revolutionary classics acquainted me with various revolutionary theories, ideologies, and problems."[5] He also reported that he became acquainted with the writings of Charles Darwin and Herbert Spencer at this time. During the four months of his imprisonment, he opined, he learned much more than he could have during a semester at the Seminary.

Because of his political activities, Sorokin was expelled from school. However, he was welcomed in revolutionary circles. He now engaged full time in political agitation among the peasants. Soon perceiving that this was a dead end, he moved to St. Petersburg, where he supported himself as a tutor. He also entered night school to prepare himself for the university. In 1909 Sorokin passed the entrance examinations and enrolled in the newly opened Psycho-Neurological Institute in which courses in sociology were given by two internationally famous scholars: M. M. Kovalevsky and E. de Roberty. He succeeded in acquiring the position of secretary and research assistant to Kovalevsky. In addition to Kovalevsky and de Roberty, other scholars from whom Sorokin took work at the Institute included Leon Petrajitsky (law), Tugan-Baranovsky (economics), N. Rosin and A. Jijilenko (criminology and penology), M. I. Rostevtzeff and N. O. Lossky (history and classics). In addition to serving as private secretary and assistant to Kovalesvsky, Sorokin also became teaching assistant to de Roberty and co-editor with him of a series of studies of *New Ideas in Sociology.*

Sorokin also stated that Petrajitsky and Bekhterev employed him as co-editors of *New Ideas in the Science of Law* and of a *Journal of Psychology and Criminal Anthropology.* Through Kovalevsky and Petrajitsky, Sorokin met leaders of the Liberal and Constitutional Democratic Parties as well as statesmen and members of the Duma. The last time he was arrested by the czarist police (1913), he was soon released through the efforts of Kovalevsky. Sorokin thus had the rare good fortune to arrive on the scene at a time when an emerging Russian social science was in its budding stage and to serve a number of notable scholars as a student assistant.

Sorokin received a fellowship to facilitate his studies for a master's degree in criminal law under N. Rosin, A. Jijilenko, and N. Lazarevsky. This appointment covering the years 1914 to 1916 permitted him to devote full time to his studies. He passed his master's oral examination in the fall of 1916, planning to submit his volume on *Crime and Punishment* (1913) for the degree of magister of criminal law. The time for public defense of his thesis was set for March, 1917. However, the onset of the Revolution made this impossible.

As the Revolution deepened and the communists came into power, conditions worsened. The government abolished scientific degrees in 1918. They were later restored, and after changes in plans and the survival of the Revolution, Sorokin offered his two-volume *System of Sociology* (1920) as a doctoral dissertation. It was defended successfully, and he was awarded the doctor of philosophy degree on April 22, 1922.

Meanwhile, the passing of his master's oral examination won Sorokin the degree of magistrant of criminal law, entitling him to become a *privat-docent* (private lecturer) paid out of student fees. In the period of 1914 to 1916 his status as a graduate student, and, later, as an instructor exempted him from service in the World War I Russian army. However, Sorokin reported that during World War I he served on committees formed to assist the mobilization of the nation's economic resources and service to the recreational and educational needs of invalids and veterans. Moreover, he delivered morale-building, patriotic lectures to military and civilian audiences.[6]

Even while engaging in such patriotic activities, however, Sorokin stated that he was occupied with others of like mind in preparing plans for the defeat of the Russian army by the Germans and for the imminent downfall of the czarist regime.[7]

The fullest report of the events of Sorokin's life during the Russian Revolution (1917–1922) is contained in his *Leaves from a Russian Diary*. His position as a lecturer at the University of St. Petersburg put him in direct touch with persons who were to play a major role in the Revolution. His membership in the Social Revolutionary Party tied his fortunes to those of the group who were to play the major role in the first phase of the Revolution. The fall of the Kerensky Provisional Government and the assumption of power by the Bolshevists radically reversed the fortunes of the moderate revolutionaries.

In March and April, 1917, Sorokin has reported, the leaders of the Social Revolutionary party decided to found a newspaper to mold public opinion in a desired direction. Sorokin was one of a committee of five appointed to serve as editors of *Delo Naroda (The Affair of the People)*, as the paper was called.[8] Because of sharp differences of opinion with the other editors, Sorokin soon resigned his position and helped to organize another Social Revolutionary paper, the *Volia Naroda (The Will of the People)*.[9]

Sorokin by no means confined his activities to newspaper editing. He stated that he was offered three posts under the provisional government: assistant minister of the interior, director of the Russian telegraphic service, and secretary to Prime Minister Kerensky. He accepted the position as Kerensky's secretary.[10] Also in his home province of Vologda, he helped organize the electoral campaign for the Constitutional Assembly. He was, thus, one of the founders of the All Russian Peasant Soviet. He reports that peasant conventions in three districts of Vologda Province unanimously nominated him as deputy. This nomination was concurred in by the Social Revolutionary Party of Vologda.[11]

When Kerensky was defeated and the Bolshiviki assumed power, Sorokin's roles as Kerensky's former secretary and as representative of the Province of Vologda became negative assets. Meanwhile, continued publication of the Social Revolutionary Party paper that he had helped organize and that he continued to serve as editor became dangerous. Sorokin wrote that his first arrest by the Bolshevists occurred in the offices of *The Will of the People* on January 2, 1918.[12]

After fifty-seven days in jail, an old friend from his early Social Revolutionary days who was now cooperating with the Bolshevists secured Sorokin's release. Upon release from prison Sorokin reported that he continued to engage in anti-Bolshevist activity with various Moscow groups. He assisted in the publication of an anti-Bolshevist newspaper *(Regeneration)*. However, when the first copy appeared, Bolshevist agents raided the office, destroyed the copy, broke up the forms and matrices, and smashed the presses. The tension between the two groups of revolutionaries continued to mount, and by the end of May, 1917, members of the Constitutional Assembly and of the League for the Regeneration of Russia who opposed the Bolshevists began to flee Moscow.

Sorokin reported that he participated in plans for an anti-Bolshevist revolt in Archangel and set out for that city. He never reached it. The Bolsheviks had learned of the revolt and put out a dragnet for the conspirators. After a period of hiding from the Bolshevist police, Sorokin decided to give himself up to the authorities. He was in prison for four months under sentence of death. There were daily executions from among his cell mates. An old student intervened for him, and Sorokin's release was secured by the direct intervention of Lenin, who wrote an article in *Pravda* urging that intellectuals such as Sorokin could be useful as educators to the new Communist order.[13]

Sorokin was permitted to return to the Psycho-Neurological Institute and was elected professor of sociology in both the Agricultural Academy and the Institute of Public Economy. Because of the extra rations, he accepted both positions. At the same time two large cooperative organizations not yet nationalized asked him to write textbooks in law and sociology.[14]

In the spring of 1920 Sorokin was transferred to the Agricultural Academy of Czarskoe Selo. Shortly after this he published his two-volume *System of Sociology* which, he stated, caused a temporary flurry among the Chekhists (secret police). Official persecutions were not systematically organized at this time but were whimsical and arbitrary, varying by the day. However, if one were picked up he could stay in jail indefinitely. Hence with the excitement over possible subversion in his *System of Sociology,* he deemed it wise to drop out of sight for a couple of weeks. As he had anticipated, the flurry died down, and he was able to submit and defend his text as his doctoral dissertation.

Sorokin witnessed the Great Famine of 1921 which brought the prestige of the Bolshevist goverment to a low ebb. In May, 1922, he published a book on *The Influence of Hunger on Human Behavior.* It was severely censored beforehand, and its appearance coincided with renewed vigor in the Soviet's propaganda campaign against opposition on the home front. Once again Sorokin thought it expedient to drop out of sight for a while. A wave of arrests of scholars was under way, but they were routinely being banished rather than executed or sent to prison. Since the police in St. Petersburg were relatively more severe, Sorokin decided to give himself up to the authorities in Moscow in the hope of banishment rather than imprisonment or execution. It all worked out as planned, and Sorokin was banished to Czechoslovakia.

In Prague he offered a series of public lectures which were published as *The Contemporary State of Russia* (Prague, 1922). He also worked up a volume of *Essays on Social Pedagogy and Politics.* He participated as editor and contributed to a journal on *The Peasant's Russia,* publishing in it a series of studies of agrarian problems. He undertook work on the manuscript that was to become his *Sociology of Revolution* (1925).

Sorokin's intellectual activities in Prague attracted the attention of international scholars. This resulted in the extension of invitations from Edward C. Hayes of the University of Illinois and from Edward A. Ross of the University of Wisconsin to come to North America and deliver a series of lectures on the Russian Revolution. After Sorokin's arrival in the United States, his predicament as a penniless *emigré* was learned by Henry Noble MacCracken, president of Vassar College. MacCracken invited him to be the guest of Vassar for a few weeks with complete freedom to study English and work up his lectures.[15]

Upon completion of his lecture series at the Universities of Wisconsin and Illinois in 1924, Sorokin was invited by F. Stuart Chapin to teach in the summer session at the University of Minnesota. His success in teaching there led to his appointment as full professor. During his six years at Minnesota, Sorokin published six works: *Leaves from a Russian Diary* (1924); *The Sociology of Revolution*

(1925); *Social Mobility* (1927); *Contemporary Sociological Theories* (1928); *Principles of Rural-Urban Sociology* (with C. C. Zimmerman, 1929); and the three volumes of *A Systematic Source-Book in Rural Sociology* (with C. C. Zimmerman and C. J. Galpin, 1930–1932).

In 1929 Sorokin was invited to deliver a series of lectures at Harvard University. These turned out to be exploratory prior to inviting him to join the faculty and establish a department of sociology. In addition to serving as chairman, Sorokin continued his program of research and writing. Harvard assisted him by financial grants (amounting to some $10,000) in securing the assistance of specialists in the history of painting, sculpture, architecture, music, literature, science, philosophy, economics, religion, ethics, law, war, and revolution. Sorokin was compiling evidence from all such areas of rates and forms of cultural change. This project, which he had conceived while still at Minnesota, eventually was published as his four-volume *Social and Cultural Dynamics.* A large part of the work in assembling material from special cultural areas was done by displaced Russian scholars. Sorokin was able both to secure excellent skills and talents at bargain prices and to assist many refugee scholars in the difficult transition period in the New World. Meanwhile, he established and strengthened the Harvard department and enhanced its attractiveness with invitations to many eminent specialists. He eventually gave up the chairmanship in 1942.

Four years after retirement from the chairmanship at Harvard, Sorokin received a letter from Eli Lilly offering him $20,000 to finance research on the topic of the moral and mental regeneration of contemporary humanity. At the suggestion of President Conant, the grant was made (for tax exemption purposes) to Harvard University, though the money was entirely at Sorokin's disposal. Using only a fraction of the fund, Sorokin produced a volume on *The Reconstruction of Humanity* (1948). Lilly was so impressed that he made an additional grant of $100,000 at the rate of $20,000 a year for the next five years. The grant led to the establishment in 1949 of the Harvard Research Center in Creative Altruism with Sorokin as director. Thereafter his time was equally divided between his teaching duties in the sociology department and directorship of the center. Ten years later, when the fund was exhausted, the Lilly Foundation granted an additional $25,000 for continuation of the work of the center and to finance publication of the Proceedings of the First International Congress for Comparative Study of Civilization, of which Sorokin was president, at Salzburg in 1961.

In April, 1950, Sorokin gave the Cole Lectures on "Recent Philosophies of History" at Vanderbilt University. These were published as

Social Philosophies of an Age of Crisis (1950). In January, 1955, he retired from teaching but continued to act as director of the Harvard Research Center in Creative Altruism until he was seventy. His publications accelerated in volume after his retirement, illustrated by *Fads and Foibles in Modern Sociology* (1956), *The American Sex Revolution* (1956), and *Power and Morality* (1959).

After his retirement from teaching Sorokin attended many national and international congresses, and he was elected the first president of the International Society for the Comparative Study of Civilizations (1961). He was elected president of the American Sociological Association in 1965.

In 1966 Sorokin returned to the special field of sociological theory for the first time since his 1928 review. It is a testimony to his flexibility and his movement toward personal synthesis that he completely scrapped his earlier typology redividing the theories into nominalistic-singularistic-atomistic, on the one hand, and systemic on the other. He located his positions, which he described as integral theory, primarily among the systemic theories, but as a more comprehensive form of theory which integrates the other two.

> In their sound parts, the singularistic-atomistic theories of social, cultural and personal congeries are reconcilable and complement the sound body of systemic theories: Each class of these theories gives a real knowledge of the singularistic and systemic forms of the total superorganic reality.[16]

Sorokin continued giving additional lecture series and working on additional publications until his death in 1968.

Sorokin's Intellectural Development

In his autobiography Sorokin undertook to trace the development of his own ideas. There is not the slightest reason to doubt the accuracy of his self-estimate. He divided his intellectual development into three phases.

Traditional Religiosity

Like many another simple peasant or artisan youth with special intellectual aptitude at the same time and place in Russia, young Sorokin had begun to climb the one major ladder up and out of his peasant-artisan background. He had won a fellowship at one of the seminaries which trained individuals for teaching or the priesthood. To win such opportunities young Sorokin had to demonstrate not only intellectual acumen but special interest in things religious. He reported that he was spellbound by the lives of the saints and took them as an ideal. He plunged intensely into activities as a youthful teacher-preacher among the peasants. At this stage of his life Sorokin stated his mentality was dominated by Russian Orthodox Christianity.

> This religious climate . . . served as a stimulus and outlet for the development of my creative propensities. . . . I learned *verbatim,* prayers, psalms, and scriptural texts as well as the details of religious services. . . . This knowledge was also partly responsible for my becoming a teacher-preacher at the neighborhood gatherings of peasants during the long winter evenings. . . . The moral precepts of Christianity, especially of the Sermon on the Mount and the Beatitudes, decisively conditioned my moral values not only in youth but for the rest of my life. . . . All in all mine was an idealistic world-view in which God and nature, truth, goodness, and beauty, religion, science, art, and ethics were all united into one harmonious system.[17]

It was the combination of intellectual acumen and traditionalistic piety which gave peasant and artisan youth in Czarist Russia access to the theological and teaching seminaries. Stalin, too, had started up this particular ladder. Traditionally such young men would have normally ended up in the village *intelligentsia* or priesthood. However, at that particular time and place the theological and teaching seminaries were becoming hotbeds of revolutionary excitement.

Positivistic Organicism

The alertness and impressionability that had led young Sorokin to isolate the religious element of his peasant artisan surroundings as its most dramatic and exciting component could hardly have remained untouched by the intoxicating atmosphere of revolution. All the evidence suggests that Sorokin gravitated immediately and spontaneously to the centers of excitement.

Inasmuch as czarist monarchism was locked together with Russian Orthodox religiosity into a traditional complex, revolutionary opposition to the regime usually had an antireligious bent. How far young Sorokin went along with this trend is indicated by what he describes as his "semi-atheistic rejection of the theologies and rituals of the Russian Orthodox Church," his abandonment of religion for science, and adherence to the czarist monarchy and capitalism for "republican, democratic, and socialist views."[18] He embraced the tenets of revolution with religious intensity and became an active missionary among worker peasant groups for his new gospel.

While the prevailing atmosphere in the Russian universities at the time Sorokin was an undergraduate was not characterized by active revolutionary ferment, it, too, differed rather markedly from the traditional religiosity of Sorokin's childhood. His most admired teachers, Kovalevsky and de Roberty, were more liberal than revolutionary. They led Sorokin to the sociological classics. In Sorokin's own estimation the result was a modification of his revolutionary inclinations toward a position close to that of such classical sociologists as Comte, Spencer, and Durkheim.

Philosophically the emerging system was a variety of empirical neo-positivism or critical realism based upon logical and empirical scientific methods. Sociologically it represented a sort of synthesis of Comteian-Spencerian sociology of evolution-progress corrected and supplemented by the theories of N. Mikhailovsky, P. Lavrov, E. de Roberty, L. Petrajitsky, M. Kovalevsky, M. Rostovtzeff, P. Kropotkin, among the Russian social thinkers, and by the theories of G. Tarde, E. Durkheim, G. Simmel, M. Weber, R. Stammler, K. Marx, V. Pareto, and other western social scientists. Politically it was a form of socialistic ideology, founded upon the ethics of solidarity, mutual aid, and freedom.[19]

Inasmuch as the classical sociologists conjoined a confidence in scientific methods as adequate to the study of society with an organismic theory of society and faith in its progress or evolution, the position has been described as positivistic organicism. Sorokin's position in his own estimation was, at this time, a form of classical theory, differing only in its socialistic coloration. "I did not," Sorokin observed, "foresee then that this 'scientific, positivistic, and progressively optimistic' *Weltanschauung* soon would be found wanting by the crucial test of historical events and would engender the second crisis in my world outlook."[20]

Integralism

In the twentieth century the naïve confidence in the classical sociological theories of progress was seriously shaken. It was difficult to reconcile wars and revolutions with the concept of progress. However, even before the close of the nineteenth century the balked aspirations of many groups were accompanied by increasing dissatisfaction with the classical synthesis of positivism, organicism, and progress. World War I and the backlash of disillusionment that accompanied the Russian Revolution delivered the final blows to the prestige of sociology's first synthesis. Indication of the state of the popular mind was the enormous popularity of Spengler's *Decline of the West*.

Sorokin characteristically attributed his own reactions to his independent assessment of world events rather than to any change in world opinion.

> Already World War I had made some fissures in the positivistic, "scientific," and humanistic *Weltanschauung* I had held before the War. The Revolution of 1917 enormously enlarged these fissures and eventually shattered this world-outlook with its positivistic philosophy and sociology, its utilitarian system of values, and its conception of historical process as a progressive evolution toward an even better man, society, and culture.[21]

Sorokin reported that the revision of his point of view was virtually complete by the end of the 1920s. "It resulted in what I now call the *integral system* of philosophy, sociology, psychology, ethics, and values."[22] Integralism, Sorokin maintained, was systematically extended and expressed in the volumes he published in the last three decades.

Sorokin's *magnum opus* in which his integralism was brought for the first time into mature synthesis was his four-volume monograph, *Social and Cultural Dynamics*, on the cultural changes in Western civilization. This project was conceived in 1929 and eventually brought to completion with the publication of the fourth volume in 1941. Sorokin believed his publications after *Dynamics* were renewed formulations and extensions of the same point of view to new calamities of the 1950s and attempts to round out his integral system of philosophy, sociology, psychology, and ethics. Such volumes as *Man and Society in Calamity* (1942), *Socio-Cultural Causality, Space and Time* (1943), *Society, Culture, and Personality* (1947), and *The Meaning of Our Crisis* (1951) are somewhat simplified formulations and popularizations of the views of *Social and Cultural Dynamics*. The numerous volumes done or supervised for the Harvard Research Center in Creative Altruism were primarily conceived as the exploration of alternatives to the decadence of contemporary culture; they were practical applications of integralist theory intended as a basis for social reconstruction.

Comte's Positivism and Sorokin's Integralism

Since by his own admission Sorokin's position in his inexperienced youth was close to that of the classical sociologists, it is not unfair to compare his views with those of the founder of sociology to see how far in fact his integralism departs from the classical formula.

Comte drew premises for his own system from both the idealistic and empiricist traditions of philosophy. The essence of human society, he believed, is constituted by ideas. Moreover, such ideas are not the isolated notions of individuals but collective formations. Comte's successor, Durkheim, built directly on Comte in this respect and made the concept of collective representations as the basic facts of society quite explicit. Comte, furthermore, did not draw a sharp distinction between society and culture. Humanity or mankind consisted of the collective mind of all men living and dead. It has an organic unity. The central clue to its unity is provided by the prevailing mode of thought of a given time and place. This mode of thought of mankind progresses through three grand stages: theological and priest-dominated, metaphysical and philosopher-dominated, and positivistic and scientist-dominated. The unity in the various aspects of mankind is displayed in the presence of the basic presuppositions of the dominant mode of thought in all the various spheres of sociocultural life: religion, economics, politics, and so on.

The similarities between Comte's position and Sorokin's integralism are numerous. Like Comte, Sorokin believed that systems and supersystems of sociocultural life form dynamic, interrelated wholes. Moreover, like Comte at the highest level (the supersystem), the lines between society and culture are blurred. The primary difference at this level between Comte and Sorokin is the latter's shift toward a vaguely theistic position. For Comte, humanity itself became the substitute for God. Integralism, according to Sorokin,

> views total reality as the infinite X of numberless qualities and quantities: spiritual and material, everchanging and unchangeable, personal and super-personal, temporal and timeless, spatial and spaceless, one and many . . . its highest center—the *summum bonum*—is the Infinite Creative X that passes all human understanding.[23]

Comte's early formulations thrust theology aside as a primitive stage in human thought. However, in the end Comte substituted humanity for God and transformed sociology into applied theology, hopelessly confusing the lines between science, philosophy, and religion. Sorokin, too, blurred the lines between these disciplines. The essence of his point of view, he urged, is the same as that of the philosophical thought of Taoism, the Upanishads, the Bhagavad-Gita, the writings of Hindu and Mahayana logicians, the Zen Buddhists, the great Muslim thinkers and poets, the philosophies of Heraclitus and Plato and to a lesser extent Aristotle, the philosophies of Plotinus, Porphyry, the Hermetic, Orphic, and Christian Church fathers and mystics and the philosophies of various rationalists.[24]

Though Comte's early system of sociology rejected religion, he came to the view that only religion was able to provide the essential unity to society. Prior to Comte's association with Saint-Simon, he seems to have accepted the traditional Catholicism in which he was reared. Sorokin, too, seems to have undergone a similar series of developments starting with traditional religious orthodoxy, becoming for a time an atheist, eventually subscribing to religion once more. Though there were differences, both Comte and Sorokin came to subscribe to nonstandard faiths: Comte to the religion of humanity, and Sorokin to an amalgam of elements drawn from the great religions and philosophies of the world.

Comparable to Comte's view that a peculiar set of ideas and methods of thought provided the order to the stages of the development of mankind is Sorokin's view that the essence of every cultural system (and, incidentally, system of ethics, religion, and philosophy) is the peculiar set of values taken as of central importance and the appropriate methods for the pursuit of these values.

> Any great culture, instead of being a mere dumping place of a multitude of diverse cultural phenomena, existing side by side and unrelated to one another, represents a unity or individuality whose parts are permeated by the same fundamental principle and articulate the same basic value. The dominant part of the fine arts and science of such a unified culture, of its philosophy and religion, of its ethics and law, of its main forms of social, economic, and political organization, of most of its mores and manners, of its ways of life and mentality, all articulate, each in its own way, this basic principle and value. This value serves as its major premise and foundation. For this reason the important parts of such an integrated culture are also interdependent causally: if one important part changes, the rest of its important parts are bound to be similarly transformed.[25]

For Comte there were three great historical systems of humanity: theological, metaphysical, and positivistic. These followed one another in a progressive series. For Sorokin, too, there were three great systems depending on the value which forms their integrating point. The two major contrasting types were the ideate, a civilization integrated around a supersensory value such as the love of God, and sensate, a civilization integrated around sensual values. Just as Comte's metaphysical society was transitional between the theological and positivistic, Sorokin's idealistic civilization was transitional between ideate and sensate.

However, while Comte's systems were thought to represent a progressive series, Sorokin emphatically rejected the concept of progress. The impetus for change in Comte's view was the application of man's intelligence to the solution of his problems and the increasing control of the emotions by reason. Sorokin, however, had no equivalent confidence in human reason or similar notion of the relation between reason and the emotions. "No finite form, either ideational or sensate, is eternal. Sooner or later it is bound to exhaust its creative abilities. When this moment comes, it begins to disintegrate and decline."[26] The basic mechanism of change for Sorokin appeared to be the property of "exhaustion of creative abilities."

For Comte the millennium was being ushered in by the application of science to social affairs, but for Sorokin the disintegration of civilization, the salient property of our epoch, was in large measure a product of the application of science. While Comte reversed the medieval philosophy of history, Sorokin in many respects returned the theory of history to a formulation closer to that of St. Augustine with whom, in fact, he was fond of identifying. The contemporary crisis of society and culture is traced to the corruption of a sensate culture in a manner that would gladden the heart of a medieval theologian. For example, contemporary art, Sorokin insisted, "is primarily a museum of social and cultural pathology. It centers in the police morgue, the criminal's hide-out, and the sex organs, operating mainly on the level of the social sewers."[27] The corruption of contemporary civilization is even manifest in its methods of thought. There has been, Sorokin maintained, "an increasing relativization of sensory truth until it becomes indistinguishable from error."[28] Society has undermined its own values "through a progressively thin and narrow empiricism divorced from other social values—religion, goodness, beauty, and the like."[29] Ultimately even science is said to have "distinctly impaired our understanding of reality."[30] In the fields of ethics and law the crisis of sensate culture is said to have resulted in transforming values into "mere 'rationalizations,' 'derivations,' or 'beautiful speech reactions,' veiling the egotistic interests, pecuniary motives, and acquisitive propensities of individuals and groups."[31] Ethical norms have ceased to be guides to behavior, becoming instead a smoke screen for lust and greed. Legal norms have been converted into devices for exploiting the weak by the powerful.

The crisis of contemporary civilization, Sorokin insisted, runs through all institutions: family, government, economic institutions, cultural institutions. Even international relations have been in crisis. Accompanying the crisis has been a rise in the rates of suicide, criminality, war, and revolution. Contemporary culture as a whole is said to be characterized by chaotic syncretism, quantitative colossalism, and the loss of creativeness.

Somewhat parallel to the manner in which St. Augustine had held out *The City of God* as an alternative to the decay of the earthly city, Sorokin held out the promise of a possible reconstruction of humanity. The remedy required "replacement of the withered root of sensate culture by an ideational or idealistic root, and eventually in a substitution of a full grown and more spiritual culture for the decadent sensate form."[32] However, despite many similarities, Hans Speier calls attention to the error of identifying Sorokin's theories too closely with those of the Church fathers. He described Sorokin's position as

> a modern vulgarization of early Christian thinking. The distinction between senses, reason, and faith is retained as a universal principle of division of the types of man, cultures, and "systems" within each culture. The hierarchization of these values, however, is blurred. The idea of a supreme good is given up in favor of a relativistic point of view, tempered by eclectic professions of absolute standards. Throughout his work some kind of hierarchy of the three values is implied, as is particularly evident from the expressions of contempt, disgust, and revulsion in which Sorokin indulges whenever he describes the "sensate sewers" of our time. However, it is not the truth of faith which ranks highest, as one might expect from familiarity with the tradition which Sorokin follows in distinguishing the three values. Rather, he "prefers" idealism to ideationalism. Again, ideationalism is constructed as a compromise between sensation and idealism, which blurs the distinctions further. Finally, the methods used in *Social and Cultural Dynamics* are those of "sensate science," which has induced a malicious critic to remark that the work may be a satire on modern social science.[33]

So long as Sorokin's analysis remained within the framework set by *Social and Cultural Dynamics,* Speier's criticism is well taken. In the end Sorokin's position remains a form of cultural relativism, for even granting that one replaces the root of sensate culture by an idealistic or ideational form, this would only be for a time. According to Sorokin's own principle, sooner or later it is bound to exhaust its creative abilities.

However, there is some possible indication that Sorokin was moving toward a conception of the final deliverance of mankind in the form of an integralistic system of civilization which is superior to the three inevitable forms (ideate, sensate, and idealistic).

> From the integralist standpoint, the present antagonism between science, religion, philosophy, ethics, and art is unnecessary, not to mention disastrous. In the light of an adequate theory of true reality and

value, they all are one and all serve one purpose: the unfolding of the Absolute in the relative empirical world, to the greater nobility of Man and to the greater glory of God. As such they should and can cooperate in the fulfillment of this greatest task.[34]

This would seem to bring Sorokin even closer to the position of the Church fathers.

In his autobiography Sorokin insisted that at least in his personal life he succeeded in "reuniting into one *summum bonum* the supreme Trinity of Truth, Goodness, and Beauty. . . . Integralism has given me a firm foundation for maintenance of my integrity and has wisely guided my conduct amidst the bloody debris of the crumbling sensate civilization."[35]

Sorokin's last book, *Sociological Theories of Today,* indicates that he had no intention of leaving integralism at the level of a purely personal philosophy. The various conceptual developments of his work were clearly being codified. The following estimate sums up the differences between his earlier and later treatments of theory.

Sorokin's earlier review of sociological theory, *Contemporary Sociological Theories* (1928), was completed prior to the synthesis of his distinctive theoretical position in his *magnum opus,* the *Social and Cultural Dynamics* (1937–1941, 4 vols.). The primary difference between the two reviews of theory, apart from the survey of new developments in sociology from 1928 to the present, is the introduction of a new classification of theories and the application of a consistent critical position to all material reviewed.

In *Sociological Theories of Today* Sorokin divides sociological theories into three types: (1) Singularistic-Atomistic, (2) Systemic—divided into Systemic theories of culture and Systemic theories of society with numerous sub-divisions—and (3) the Integral System of structural and dynamic Sociology. Much of the material earlier contained in *Fads and Foibles in Modern Sociology* (1956) is summarized under the Singularistic-Atomistic type of theory. Most of the recent developments in the theory of culture and society are subsumed under Systemic types of theory. There is, apparently, only one true example of Integral theory, namely, Sorokin's own. Integral theory is claimed to synthesize whatever is valuable in all other methodologies and substantive theories, bringing the methods and values of the senses, the reason and intuition, and the interpretations of corresponding forms of personality, society, and supersystems—cultures and civilizations—in which these various methods and values are embodied into balanced perspective.

All new major developments in sociology since the 1920's are reviewed to determine the extent to which they are false or redundant, that is the extent to which they disagree or agree with the Integral System of Sociology.[36]

Sociological Theories of Today leaves little doubt that Sorokin was bringing the diverse strands of his thought into unity.

Soldier of Fortune

The nearest counterparts to Sorokin's system of ideas are found in Hegel in philosophy and Comte in sociology. Sorokin's writing has a vigorous and forthright character and is inspired by a zest for the destruction of popular idols. He often conveyed the impression of rather naïve heedlessness, and many a person had been lured into battle only to discover himself vis-à-vis with a battle-wise campaigner. One often discovered that Sorokin was able to quote chapter and verse from his writings apparently in direct refutation of charges which a moment before had seemed almost self-evident.[37]

Although Sorokin appeared to have a unified system of ideas, unity was provided by the Absolute which, in principle, is placed outside manifest experience as an ultimate reality not directly accessible except by intuition. The Absolute comprises all dynamisms, all changes, all contradictions, which arise in the unfolding experiences of everyday life.

Sorokin conceived of the senses, the mind, and the spirit as three basic realities, each with its special form of knowledge and truth. The three methods comprise the empirical methods of science, the logical methods of reason, and the intuitive methods of the spirit. Each of the three basic realities supplies its distinctive value to human endeavor: the sensory, the value of reason, and the super-rational, super-empirical value of faith. On the basis of these three types of value, meaning, and truth, Sorokin projected the existence of distinctive types of civilization and personality (men of science, men of reason, and men of faith).

In examining the manner in which various social and cultural phenomena are related to one another, Sorokin apparently subscribed to a holistic position. In fact, he described himself on occasion as a holist. Holism is inseparable from the view that in some sense the whole is a causal component in the development and change of its parts. In this connection, the exchange between Louis Schneider[38] and Sorokin is of special interest.[39] Quite in accord with the assumption that Sorokin's concept of sociocultural systems was holistic, Schneider saw him as accounting for change primarily on the basis of an internal dialect (that is, change is brought about by the structure of the socio-cultural system itself without any requirement of extra-system factors). While Sorokin did not altogether accept Schneider's interpretation, he agreed that he accounted for change primarily in dialectical terms.

While Sorokin's holism appeared to be complete in every respect, whenever he was criticized for failing to account for various categories of events which failed to obey his principles, he was able simply to point out that he had insisted that not all sociocultural phenomena are integrated into supersystems. There also are partly organized systems, contradictory systems, and collections of elements that form mere congeries without any system at all. Hence one was left quite in the dark as to when Sorokin's holism would or would not apply, and he was free to use or not use it as he moved from case to case and from argument to argument.

Treating the objects of sense experience, of logical reasoning, of faith as three categories of reality, each with its appropriate methods of study (scientific empiricism, logical reasoning, and intuition), seems very plausible in terms of various ancient notions of human thought and experience. However, whenever one considers the actual reasoning processes of men, this treatment of these as equal and parallel forms of truth establishment leads to considerable confusion. In actual cases of scientific investigation various empirical, logical, and intuitive (in some senses of this highly ambiguous term) elements are simultaneously present. To treat the intuitions and revelations of mystics as in some sense parallel to the deductions of a logician or the experimental investigations of a scientist is to blur very significant differences between them and in no way to solve the problem that arises when, for example, the suggestions of intuition are in direct contradiction with the other so-called modes of truth establishment. On the other hand, to ignore such contradictions and, perhaps, assign them to the Absolute in which all contradictions are ultimately resolved, is to solve the problem by irrational means.

Sorokin's procedure of placing the three so-called realities on a parallel plane (objects of sense, reason, and faith) leveled down the distinction between values and facts. This in turn became a license to load his writing with all sorts of supercharged value judgments. Moreover, he was simultaneously left free to pursue any tack he pleased and did not hesitate, for example, to quantify all sorts of matters which even some rather extreme positivists found rather hair-raising while attacking attempts at measurement and quantification by other researchers. Riley and Moore, for example, observe:

... notwithstanding his continuing concern with problems of measuring qualitative variables, he ridicules as "metrophrenia" the solutions to these problems worked out by serious and competent scholars. His gratuitous attack on Guttman scaling, for example, serves only to demonstrate his fundamental misunderstanding of the meaning of scalability and his own failure to recognize the procedure as an important complement to his own work. Thus the reader can find passages in his critical writings which seem to support almost any standpoint—or its opposite![40]

Sorokin described his political position as that of a "conservative, Christian anarchist."[41] Presumably his anarchism (which ordinarily is an intransigent form of individualism) coexisted without any sense of conflict with his holism (which is ordinarily an intransigent form of collectivism). Sorokin's "conservativism" also apparently coexisted without conflict with his "nonconformism" and "revolutionism." He was, in fact, inordinately proud of his "idiosyncrasies" and his "bullheadedness and deviationism."[42] Finally, his Christianity coexisted with the lack of any church affiliation and the inclination to pick and choose bits at will from any religion or philosophy that interested him.

As many a person has discovered, the farther one goes in Sorokin's writing in the attempt to work out its internal system, the more certain he is to encounter difficulties or to become bogged down in its quicksands. This resistance to systematization, in fact, seems to be the basic reason why Sorokin has never become the founder of a school. Despite its pungent slogans and battle cries, his integralism resists the kind of codification into a dogma which is so critical for school formation. At the same time, the very property of Sorokin's thought which made it unusable for purposes of sect formation emphasizes the striking fact that in his hands his set of notions constituted an unusually effective instrument.

All these considerations suggest that the ordinary modes of estimating bodies of theory do not apply to Sorokin's integralism. At the same time, the judgment that, despite all the many genuine insights that Sorokin scattered so liberally throughout his work, his ideas were in fact an eclectic patch and paste collage, though in a sense correct, seems also to miss the point. The one estimate that seems best to fit the complex of notions that constituted Sorokin's integralism is that *they were the arsenal of a soldier of fortune.*

Sorokin himself represented his life as "a sort of continuous 'wayfaring' through most different occupational, social, economic, cultural, political, and ethnic positions and group affiliations."[43] After the loss of his mother when Sorokin was three, he was taken with his father and elder brother on their itinerant route from village to village. After the break with their father, the two boys (aged ten and fourteen) were able to maintain themselves in the same itinerant trade. Adeptness at taking advantage of the opportunities around him made it possible for Sorokin to obtain as good an education as was available to a youth on the Russian frontier. He was also able to start on the route up and out of his peasant-artisan background through the teaching seminary. The same acceptance and eye for the main chance guided Sorokin in his participation in the two Russian revolutions with his imprisonment three times by the czarist government and three times by the communist government. He managed to found departments of sociology at Leningrad, the stronghold of communism, and Harvard, the intellectual stronghold of capitalism. Sorokin summed up his own individualistic adaptability as follows:

> Sternly disciplined for many years in this sort of school, I became, to a notable degree, a self-reliant, independent, now and then nonconformist individual who in his search for truth does not accept any authority, any theory, any belief, or any value until it is tested and verified by all the relevant evidence available.[44]

Since Sorokin's list of the various forms of truth included the empirical, the rational, and the intuitive, he was quite free to accept or reject just about anything he pleased, unworried about contradictions, since in the Absolute, which includes everything, all contradictions are resolved. The truth of this last notion is apparently given in intuition.

Sorokin was one of the types cast up by revolution, a soldier of fortune, an ideologist produced by successive displacements (from peasant-artisan to seminary student; from potential candidate for the church school or clergy to revolution; from revolutionary to servant of Bolshevism; from servant of Bolshevism to celebrated American professor of sociology). He managed to survive these successive displacements with a combination of skill, intelligence, and good fortune. He became increasingly adept in the techniques of ideological combat. He came, also, to locate his objectives in himself alone. In short, Sorokin became sociology's primeval rebel without a cause, its revolutionary without a revolution.

As a warrior of a primitive type, Sorokin was an individual fighter rather than the disciplined member of a combat team. Moreover, as a primitive warrior he early learned to live off the land. Few sociologists have been more adept in exploiting every personal experience for publication purposes. Thrown into prison for anti-czarist activities, Sorokin came into contact with a variety of ordinary and political criminals and turned the experience into intellectual assets.

> They were largely responsible for the topic of my first book, *Crime and Punishment, Service and Reward* (published in 1913) and for my choice of criminology and penology . . . as the field of my first specialization at the University of St. Petersburg.[45]

After surviving arrest by the communists and being permitted to teach at St. Petersburg, Sorokin accepted the commission to write a *System of Sociology*,[46] which he used as his Ph.D. dissertation (1920).

The great Russian famine of 1921 apparently convinced Sorokin, along with many others, that the Bolshevist regime could not survive. At the same time and with typical economy, he made sociological capital of his observations of the famine with a book on *The Influence of Hunger on Human Behavior: on Social Life and Social Organization* (1921). Had Sorokin been correct in his assumption that the famine was about to bring down the Bolshevist regime, this book would probably have been a major life raft to survive the currents of change.

> Not much scientific knowledge did I gain in those twenty days I spent in the famine regions, but the memory of what I saw and heard there made me absolutely fearless in denouncing the Revolution and the monsters who were devouring Russia.[47]

However, Sorokin and various others who had assumed the imminent downfall of the Bolshevists had underestimated the extent to which the regime had made itself crisis-proof. The Bolshevists met the crisis by ruthlessly stamping out all forms of revolt and stepping up their propaganda campaign. Sorokin reported:

> In May, 1922, my book, "The Influence of Hunger on Human Behavior" . . . began to be printed. Before publication, many paragraphs, indeed whole chapters, were cut by the censors. The book as a whole was ruined, but what remained was better than nothing. The Soviets' "war on the ideological front" and terror were now being diffused with great energy. We all lived from hand to mouth, expecting some new blow each day.[48]

This is a considerable switch from being "absolutely fearless in denouncing the monsters who were devouring Russia."

The currents of revolution have a way of successively tossing now one, now another group, to leadership. As conflict grows more severe, violence may increase and the executioners of yesterday become the victims of today. However, the top ranks of leadership are in most imminent danger of being cut down. Members of lower ranks enjoy some flexibility in changing allegiance. Sorokin's survival of earlier crises was a product not only of luck and skill but of the fact that he was still of relatively minor importance among the revolutionaries. He reported that his younger brother was arrested primarily because he was brother of "Communist Enemy No. 1." This judgment, however, came not from the headquarters of the Bolshevist Party, but from "the local authorities."[49] However, in becoming a professor and author and founder of a sociology department, Sorokin's status was rising. He was well aware of the fact that this time the outcome of arrest and imprisonment could be quite different. He reported that he chose to deliver himself up to the authorities in Moscow in hopes of banishment.[50]

Escaping from Communism, Sorokin again demonstrated his capacity to capitalize on his experience. He immediately began to establish himself in Czech intellectual circles by delivering a series of lectures on Russia under the Revolution, and he turned his experiences as an editor and propagandist to account by editing and contributing to a journal on *The Peasants' Russia (Krestianskaiya Rossia)*. Sorokin's *Contemporary Situation of Russia (Sovremennoie sostoianie Rossii*, 1922) and *Popular Essays in Social Pedagogics and Politics (Popularnuye echerki sozialnoi pedagogiki i politiki*, 1922) were immediate products of this activity. His *Leaves from a Russian Diary* (1924, 1950) and *Sociology of Revolution* (1925) were started at this time though not finished until later. His writing and lecturing on the state of Russian society attracted internationally minded American sociologists, leading to the invitation to lecture on the subject in the United States.

Sorokin's transition to North America and his sojourn in the midwest were accomplished with characteristic adeptness. In the American midwest the empirical and practical aspects of American sociology were in rapid evolution. Under Minnesota influences Sorokin strengthened the positivistic aspects of his sociology, even trying his hand at sociological experimentation and developing an enthusiasm for quantifying all sorts of data. Similarly, Sorokin enthusiastically entered the emerging subdiscipline of rural sociology, making contributions in his *Principles of Rural-Urban Sociology* (1929) and his *Systematic Source Book in Rural Sociology* (1930–1932). In making the transition to America, it had been necessary for Sorokin to educate himself in western and American sociology. With characteristic efficiency he converted necessity into virtue, producing his *Contemporary Sociological Theories* (1928) which long remained the standard synthesis in the area. The work was translated into German,

French, Polish, Czech, Chinese, Turkish, Portuguese, Hindi, and, in part, into Japanese. Also during his years in the midwest, Sorokin responded to the universal American concern with self-improvement by a ground-breaking study of *Social Mobility* (1927).

At the time of his move to the American midwest, Sorokin seems to have arrived at the final adjustment of his life formula. All throughout his life Sorokin had displayed an unusual sensitivity to the dominant elements in his environment. One can only speculate on the extent to which elements of the milieu of the American midwest were components in this life formula. There are some points of major coincidence.

The milieu of the American midwest in the 1920s was characterized by its individualism, its faith in practicality (which in social science was manifest by its positivism and faith in empirical methods), and its undertone of fundamentalistic religiosity. (Sorokin had come to the Bible Belt.) Something comparable to all of these elements entered intimately into Sorokin's personal synthesis. While he had never foregone his holism with respect to sociocultural phenomena, in his personal life he appeared to have become an anarchist at this time. Moreover, quite in accord with the persistent midwestern liberal's suspicion of "bigness" at this time, Sorokin did not seem to abandon the view from the 1920s to his death that all top political authority is suspect, for power corrupts (manifest in *Power and Morality*, 1959).

One may speculate, moreover, that the influence of the strong empiricist traditions and concern with quantification in the 1920s lay at the source of Sorokin's enthusiasm for quantifying data of all types. Furthermore, Sorokin seemed to have shifted away at this time from what he described as his semi-atheistic middle period toward a more religious point of view. Perhaps the omnipresence of the undertone of fundamentalistic religiosity of the Bible Belt played a role in this partial return to the point of view of his childhood. In any case, from this time forward Sorokin always had an appreciative audience among Protestant clergymen. When he counterposed the ethic of the Sermon on the Mount to the spiral of degradation leading at last to the sensate sewers of the West, he awakened a responsive echo in fundamentalistic American circles.

Sorokin's Self-Image and Self-Presentation

Sorokin's explicit pride in his accomplishments has often been taken by his opponents as evidence of megalomania. Even a former student and academic assistant writing Sorokin's obituary expressed strong ambivalence at this aspect of Sorokin's personality.

> No man who writes two autobiographies (*Leaves from a Russian Diary* —1924, revised in 1950, and *A Long Journey*—1963) can be said to be wholly self-effacing. Sorokin was not. . . . No man who published as many books and articles as Sorokin did—in at least three original languages and countless translations—could be successfully accused of reticence. No man could, with self-activated provocation, lash out at what he regarded as sociological idiocies and would write and publish so intemperate a book as *Fads and Foibles in Modern Sociology and Related Sciences* (1956) could be thought of as having a solely dispassionate sense of the scientific enterprise. . . . In *Sociological Theories of Today* (1966), Sorokin's most extensive, negative criticism is heaped on his most respected peer, the late Georges Gurvitch of the Sorbonne. Robert K. Merton, Sorokin's most cherished former student and one-time collaborator, also gets paternal or avuncular whacks in full measure.[51]

But to take such actions as megalomania is to miss the fact that Sorokin was first and last a warrior, not of the disciplined, reticent variety who fights in the ranks, but a lone hero as in the Greek heroic period. Primitive men of war of this type have rarely been modest about their accomplishments, nor have they been less effective when they have boasted of their prowess. It is from this standpoint that Sorokin's statements illustrated by the following must be understood.

> Since I actively participated in and directly observed two world wars and two revolutions, with their disastrous results—great famines, devastating epidemics, and other calamities—it is comprehensible why these phenomena attracted my attention and became the topics of my investigations.[52]

> Having been imprisoned three times by the tsarist government and three times by the communist government, and having come in contact inside prisons, not only with political prisoners but also with non-political criminals, I naturally became interested in the phenomena of crime, criminals, and punishment.[53]

> Since my early boyhood, being incessantly confronted with a multitude of human problems, beginning with the problem of procuring means of subsistence. . . . I could not help becoming interested in human beings and in social and cultural problems.[54]

> Since I came out of the lowest peasant-labor stratum and had a full share of hardships and disenfranchisement common to such strata, I naturally identified myself with these classes and eventually became disrespectful toward the incapable, privileged, rich, and ruling groups.[55]

I was able [upon receiving a fellowship at the university] to give all my time to preparation for master's examinations as well as to my sociological research. With youthful vigor I earnestly devoted myself to these tasks, and in a record period of two years, instead of the usual four or more years, I succeeded in passing my master's oral examinations in October-November, 1916. Perhaps it should be stressed again that these examinations were much more rigorous than the American oral examinations for the Ph. D. degree.[56]

So far as the quantity of my output for these six years [at Minnesota] was concerned, I was satisfied; I knew that it exceeded the life-time productivity of the average sociologist—American or foreign.[57]

This is only a sample of the typical ways in which Sorokin publicly accounted for his achievements. To treat such statements as megalomania is to miss all the fun and excitement of sitting spellbound as the old warrior holds forth.

The Chance, Love, and Logic of the Warrior

If one takes Sorokin as a primitive warrior, a complex of factors in his writing and career which have often seemed to defy explanations may be seen to form a syndrome. He had been and continued until his death to be enormously productive; yet he did not appear to be driven by some inner compulsion or haunted by some "complex." He did not discriminate between his critics but was as inclined to thunder at minor ones as at major ones. He had a peculiar orientation toward chance.

Sorokin's profession was ideological warfare. This profession emerged out of a succession of experiences, not as a psychological complex but as a way of life. In the final form this ideological combat assumed, Sorokin's opponent became the secular drift of Western civilization. The only thing to be salvaged from this universal decay was his own point of view. He liked, as noted, to describe himself as a conservative Christian anarchist.

I did not join any of the existing parties. . . . Although a religious man in my own way, I did not join any institutionalized religion. Neither did I share the enthusiasm of various sports-fans and devotees of passing social fads and fashions. In all these and other respects I was rather an independent nonconformist with my own theories, beliefs, standards, and values which I regard as truer, more universal, and more perennial than the transitory, local, and largely obsolescent values and ideologies of many of my colleagues and students.[58]

In short, in a world of almost universal decay, Sorokin decided to be a world sufficient unto himself.

Here, at once, is a clue both to Sorokin's enormous productivity and the fascination of his activities. Ideological combat is more than an instrument to an end; it is a way of life. In its eventual form, his "battle" assumed an attack on the secular drift of contemporary civilization. As the apparently endless stream of Sorokin's writings indicated, there was little danger of his running out of subject matter. Furthermore, since nothing will draw a crowd more quickly than a fight, Sorokin's writings never failed to arouse interest. Since in the end Sorokin was promoting no cause other than his own, he put on an enormously good show and hurt no one permanently.

The type of primitive warrior who defined combat as the important thing rather than its results tends not to draw the line between opponents who are or are not worthy of their weapons. This seems to explain the fact that Sorokin tended to turn his thunder on minor as well as on major critics. He slashed back in this manner at the critics of *Fads and Foibles* and still grumbled about the matter in his autobiography.

> Despite this "backwash" [of unsympathetic reactions by critics], the criticisms of the *Fads and Foibles* have not been wholly ineffective. They seem to have tangibly influenced a number of American and foreign sociologists, psychologists, and psychiatrists. A few years later, in a somewhat simplified form, most of my criticisms were reiterated by C. Wright Mills in his book, *Sociological Imagination*. In his personal letter to me, written soon after publication of my volume, he expressed his high evaluation and essential agreement with most of my conclusions. (For one reason or another, he did not mention my volume at all in his book, which in fact was noted and adversely commented upon by the reviewer of Mill's book in the *London Times Literary Supplement*.)[59]

In 1960 Sorokin was invited to deliver the main address at the Centenary Celebration of Herbert Spencer by the president of the American Sociological Association. He then submitted the address for publication in the *American Sociological Review*, only to receive a rejection from Harry Alpert, then its editor. In his autobiography Sorokin reproduced both the letter of rejection from Alpert and his description of Alpert to a friend.

> As an office administrator he has been doing well. Now he is a dean of the graduate school of Oregon University. As a scholar he is just a third-class sociologist, who, so far as I know, wrote only one poor book about Durkheim.[60]

Many persons have found it difficult to reconcile the image of a world-famous scholar of enormous productivity with the tendency to thunder at minor and insignificant critics, to take issue over the absence of reference to his work, or to blast at the editor who dared reject his writings. There has been a misleading tendency to identify such behavior with imbalance, but this is to miss altogether the kind of warrior he was. The question of finding opponents worthy of his weapons was simply irrelevant.

Sorokin also had considerable belief in luck. Of Lilly's unexpected and unsolicited offer of money to finance his research on altruism, Sorokin observed:

> Throughout my life I have often experienced this sort of "luck" from unanticipated sources in the moments of my urgent, sometimes even desperate need. In this sense I can repeat Gandhi's remark: "When every hope is gone I find that help arrives somehow, from I know not where."[61]

Like every primitive warrior, Sorokin was deeply concerned with the nature and quality of his "luck."

How far the mark is missed when Sorokin's enormous productivity is attributed to some inner compulsion or complex, when his boasting about his achievements is conceived as megalomania, when his blasting at insignificant critics is seen as imbalance and lack of judgment, when his belief in his luck is interpreted as "mysticism." He had, rather, the firm, well-structured ego of an individualistic warrior. The personality was extroverted rather than introverted. The one thing intolerable for this type of warrior was to retire from the battle.

Sorokin's style was that of a wily combat ideologist. It had vigor rather than grace, poetic imaginativeness, or scientific economy. It often had a directness or bluntness. Sorokin, for example, liked to describe himself as "bullheaded" in the forthright manner of a man quick to admit his faults. However, it was notable that any number of synonyms, such as "stubborn," "intransigent," or "ornery," were avoided. None of these terms had quite the same capacity to disarm the opposition while, in fact, giving nothing away. Similarly, all sorts of contemporary cultural phenomena were denounced as "social sewers," disposing of these phenomena with blunt instruments. Sorokin was a rough antagonist.

There are some similarities between the styles of Sorokin and C. Wright Mills, as is to be expected, since both were assault technologists. But where Mills was a rebel, Sorokin was an old-fashioned warrior type. Sorokin's style lacked Mills' note of stridency; it was more inventive, more complex.

The movement of Sorokin's writing had a different rhythm and pattern from that of Mills'. Mills sought a weakness, striking at it with hit-and-run tactics. Sorokin made a relatively full reconnaissance of his objective. He carefully laid down a strategy and, incidentally, planned a defense and retreat route. When he was ready he mounted an offensive on the central fortifications.

Mysterious are the ways of destiny which brought Sorokin from the frontiers of northern Russia and the late nineteenth century to the pinnacle of sociology in America in the twentieth. He made enduring contributions to the discipline in virtually founding half a dozen of its subareas. Perhaps at some future time he will be seen as the last great figure of sociology's heroic age.

Notes

1. C. Wright Mills, *Power, Politics, and People*, ed. Irving Louis Horowitz (New York: Ballantine Books, 1964), p. 632.

2. Pitirim A. Sorokin, *A Long Journey* (New Haven, Conn.: College and University Press, 1963), pp. 248–49.

3. Ibid., p. 41.

4. Ibid., p. 44.

5. Ibid., p. 46.

6. Ibid., pp. 97 ff.

7. Ibid., p. 98.

8. Pitirim A. Sorokin, *Leaves from a Russian Diary* (New York: E. P. Dutton, 1924), p. 30.

9. Ibid., p. 41.

10. Ibid., p. 73.

11. Ibid., p. 83.

12. Ibid., p. 117.

13. Ibid., p. 202.

14. Ibid., p. 212.

15. *A Long Journey*, pp. 210 ff.

16. Pitirim A. Sorokin, *Sociological Theories of Today* (New York: Harper & Row, 1966), p. 646.

17. Ibid., pp. 40–41.

18. Ibid., p. 44.

19. Ibid., p. 75.

20. Ibid., p. 76.

21. Ibid., p. 204.

22. Ibid., p. 205.

23. Pitirim A. Sorokin, "Integralism Is My Philosophy," in *This Is My Philosophy,* ed. Whit Burnett (New York: Harper, 1957), p. 180.

24. Pitirim A. Sorokin, "Reply to My Critics," in *Pitirim A. Sorokin in Review,* ed. Philip J. Allens (Durham, N.C.: Duke University Press, 1963), p. 373.

25. Pitirim A. Sorokin, *The Crisis of Our Age* (New York: E. P. Dutton, 1957), p. 17.

26. Ibid., p. 28.

27. Ibid., p. 67.

28. Ibid., p. 116.

29. Ibid., p. 124.

30. Ibid., p. 125.

31. Ibid., p. 157.

32. Ibid., pp. 321–22.

33. Hans Speier, *Social Order and the Risks of War* (New York: George W. Stewart, 1952), pp. 211–12.

34. Sorokin, *Crisis of Our Age,* pp. 317–18.

35. *A Long Journey,* p. 325.

36. Don Martindale, review of *Sociological Theories of Today,* in *The Annals,* March 1967, p. 176.

37. Recent examples appear in the Allen volume, *Pitirim A. Sorokin in Review.*

38. Louis Schneider, "Toward Assessment of Sorokin's View of Change," in *Explorations in Social Change,* ed. George K. Zollschan and Walter Hirsch (Boston: Houghton Mifflin, 1964), pp. 371–400.

39. Pitirim A. Sorokin, "Comments on Schneider's Observations and Criticism," ibid., pp. 401–31.

40. Matilda White Riley and Mary E. Moore, "Sorokin's Use of Sociological Measurement," in *Sorokin in Review,* ed. Allen, p. 223.

41. In *Sorokin in Review,* ed. Allen, p. 34.

42. Ibid., p. 35.

43. Ibid., p. 31.

44. Ibid., pp. 35–36.

45. *Sorokin in Review,* ed. Allen, p. 23.

46. *Leaves from a Russian Diary,* p. 212.

47. *A Long Journey,* p. 191.

48. Ibid.

49. Ibid., p. 26.

50. Ibid., p. 193.

51. Wilbert E. Moore, "Pitirim A. Sorokin, In Memoriam," *The American Sociologist* 3, no. 2 (May 1968): 158.

52. *Sorokin in Review,* ed. Allen, p. 32.

53. Ibid.

54. Ibid.

55. Ibid., p. 34.

56. Ibid., p. 89.

57. Ibid., p. 224.
58. Ibid., p. 258.
59. Ibid., p. 297.
60. Ibid., p. 304.
61. Ibid.

Selected Bibliography

Pitirim A. Sorokin's Writings

The American Sex Revolution. Boston: Porter Sargent, 1957.

Contemporary Sociological Theories. New York: Harper & Brothers, 1927.

Fads and Foibles in Modern Sociology and Related Sciences. Chicago: Henry Regnery, 1956.

Leaves from a Russian Diary. New York: E. P. Dutton, 1924.

A Long Journey. New Haven, Conn.: College and University Press, 1963.

Power and Morality, with Walter A. Lunden. Boston: Porter Sargent, 1959.

Principles of Rural Urban Sociology, with C. C. Zimmerman. New York: Henry Holt, 1929.

Social and Cultural Dynamics. New York: American Book Co., 1937–1941.

Social Mobility. New York: Harper & Brothers, 1927.

Society, Culture, and Personality. New York: Harper & Brothers, 1947.

Sociological Theories of Today. New York: Harper & Row, 1966.

5

Theory in a
Post-Heroic Age

Since Talcott Parsons is the last of the surviving heroes of sociology
of the postwar period, it was, perhaps, inevitable that his retirement
from active teaching would raise the question of the survival of
sociology itself. Reinhold put the matter as follows:

> As he steps aside, sociology today seems to many to be in great flux,
> perhaps even disarray. There is no central focus like that provided by
> Parsonian theory. But despite the decline in interest in theory, Professor
> Parsons, the son of a Congregational minister, remains sanguine.
> "I am rather optimistic," he said. "We do not have very much what
> you could call highly publicity worth stuff coming out, but we might be
> on the threshold of quite major theoretical developments."[1]

Despite his official optimism, an optimism perhaps dictated by his
role as contemporary American sociology's foremost elder citizen,
Parsons agrees with Reinhold that there has, in fact, been a decline
in interest in theory.

The judgment by Reinhold and Parsons that there is such a decline
takes the Parsonian type of conceptual system as its standard. So
powerful was the role played by Parsonianism in the postwar American social sciences that a considerable number of other social scien-

tists also share this view. The assumption that by social theory one means a Parsonian type synthesis has led insiders like Edward Shils to the view that Parsonianism was not simply one more voice in the babel of voices, but the authoritative voice for whatever is most progressive in American society.

> The sociological theory that grows from the theory of action is simply a more forward part of a widespread consensual collectivity. Its cognitive elaboration is certainly richer and profounder than the consensual sensibility of the ordinary intelligent, educated person; its scope is broader; it is more articulate. But it is a development from the same matrix and, in its elaboration, it does not renounce its origins.
>
> The sociological theory that is self-interpretive has its correlate in the practice of collective self-control.[2]

This same assumption, i.e., that theory is to be measured by its approximation to a Parsonian type of conceptual system, also has been made by such indefatigable critics of Parsons as Alvin W. Gouldner. Gouldner not only wrote a major book with primary intent of overthrowing Parsonianism but described the revolt he was seeking to promote as a crisis, not simply for structure-functionalism, but for sociology itself. "Functional theory, and Academic Sociology more generally, are now in the early stages of a continuing crisis."[3]

The crisis of Western sociology, according to Gouldner, is manifest in a trend toward convergence of Parsonianism and Marxism, by an alienation from Parsonianism of many young sociologists, by an increasing volume of criticism of Parsonianism, by conscious attempts to develop alternatives to it, and by the appearance among many young sociologists of an interest in the values of freedom and equality rather than in the Parsonian value of order. Gouldner argues furthermore that three major forces have contributed to the crisis of Parsonianism and with it sociology itself: the emergence of new interests among sociologists who would formerly have been drawn to Parsonianism, a tendency on the part of Parsonians to dissipate their forces and, finally, the development of the United States into a welfare state to which Parsonianism was incompletely adapted.[4]

Quite apart from the correctness or incorrectness of Gouldner's charges, it is noteworthy that he shares with Shils the assumption that sociological theory is coextensive with the existence of a unified system of thought of Parsonian type. The dispute between Shils and Gouldner concerns Shils' belief that Parsonianism is, and Gouldner's belief it is not, the most advanced aspect of a "widespread consensual collectivity."

If one accepts as plausible the hypothesis that for Parsons and his followers and for many other social scientists as well, sociological theory is, or at least ought to be, a socially integrating body of belief, many otherwise baffling aspects of Parsons' work and of its reception fall into place. This may be seen in any of Parsons' works, for example, *Politics and Social Structure.* The following excerpts from a review of the book may serve as examples:

The preoccupation with distinctions in multiples of four can be endlessly illustrated from Parsons' work. There are said to be four action systems: cultural systems, social systems, personality systems, and systems of the behavioral organism. All action systems are said to have four functions: pattern maintenance, integration, goal-attainment, and adaptation. The basic functions of society operate through subsystems. The adaptive subsystem constitutes an economy. The goal attainment subsystem comprises a polity. Pattern maintenance and integration also constitute subsystems which have not been named as yet. Each subsystem is said to have a symbolic media which circulates in the hierarchy of control. These are: for the adaptive subsystem (the economy), money; for the goal attainment subsystem (the polity), power; for the pattern maintenance subsystem, commitments; for the integrative subsystem, influence.

Society for Parsons is the great system. Political activity carried on by the polity constitutes a societal subsystem carrying out the function of goal attainment. The means of goal attainment is power. Parson's argument is that all societal subsystems are identical in constitution and function and he uses the economy as the analogical model for interpreting the polity. Power is to the polity what money is to the economy. An elaborate series of analogies are drawn between the operations of money and power, and we learn that power can be "invested," "banked," "made the foundations of credit operations," and is subject to "inflationary and deflationary spirals." An identical set of analogies is applied to the nature and operations of commitments and influence.

It is my firm conviction that because of its essential scholasticism Parsonianism cannot be refuted. He cannot be refuted empirically, for empirical matters occur only incidentally by way of illustration. If one accepts the method of polarizing and dichotomizing all possibilities, one will at best generate endless terminological distinctions. One does not obtain a deepened sense of the ambiguities and confusions of the world but peace of mind when one yields one's intellect to the demand for purely formal rationality. One does not refute a scholasticism, but abandons it for a different set of objectives. In this connection one can only be moved by the manner in which Parsons ends the volume.

Contemporary social science seems to be involved in another version of the old macro-micro-argument. There are those, like George Homans, who contend that a full clarification of the "elementary forms" of social behavior is the most solid foundation on which to build social science theory and perhaps that everything else should wait. Contrary to this has been the immense flowering, in both political science and sociology, of macroscopic work, extending conspicuously into the comparative and evolutionary fields.

I do not think that there is an ultimate conflict between these two emphases. Perhaps, however, for political science in its increasingly intimate relations with sociology, the macroemphasis presents, in the present state of development of the social sciences as a whole, a special opportunity for major theoretical advance. This is not to the exclusion of the contributions of the microemphasis, but suggests that undue neglect of this opportunity might result in a serious retardation of the scientific potentials of our fields. (p. 522)[5]

Visualized in Shils' terms as the spearhead of a widespread consensual collectivity, the types of formulations represented by *Politics and Social Structure* are comparable in intent to the scholasticism of Thomas Aquinas. Both thinkers were proposing to consolidate a collectivity. The collectivity Aquinas proposed to sustain and defend was the medieval church embattled by disintegrating forces of the Western city; the collectivity Parsons proposes to sustain is American society which the conservative mind viewed as harassed by dissidents from within and threatened by international communism from without. The primary purpose of social theory from this point of view is to bring social order out of chaos. This is not a startlingly new concept of social theory, but a notion as old as Comte.

Parsons' conception of his role is not new, but what is remarkable is how far he has been able to go in realizing it. Parsons' outstanding ability and unflagging work ethic are beyond question. Also there is no doubt about his personal charm, his loyalty to his associates and students, his conventional liberalism and overall programatic conservativism. However, by themselves these things hardly account for Parsons' status.

> . . . Talcott Parsons has achieved an almost immortal status as a man of thought.
>
> Even younger sociologists, many of whom differ with him sharply about sociology, accord him a religious-like reverence before going on to do things their own way, much the way Italian Catholics genuflect before the Pope and then vote Communist.
>
> "Everybody has got to kneel and make a sign of the cross before him," said one former student. "Talcott Parsons is a god whom it is okay to take a potshot at."[6]

Parsons' position at Harvard (the most prestigious institution of higher education in the United States) is hardly sufficient to account for his influence. Other sociologists at Harvard of at least equal ability have not won equivalent status. Moreover, Parsons admittedly has no mass appeal. Nevertheless, he was destined to become a sociologist's sociologist, an enigmatic figure whom few people would claim to understand completely, an oracle who presided over the inner sanctum mediated to the outside world by a prestigious circle of trusted interpreters.

The hypothesis is advanced that the position of unparalleled authority of Parsonianism in postwar American sociology was a product of a happy coincidence of Parsons' personal traits and the needs of American intellectuals at this particular time. The United States had emerged from the war as a mass society and as the world's most powerful nation. It has been a major problem of American intellectuals to digest the implications of these facts. In American internal affairs the point of gravity had shifted decisively to the national arena and the institutions which served the wider society rather than the localities; there was a new emphasis on big government, big business, mass communications, mass advertising, mass marketing. Even in the field of socialization the large-scale organization became the rule —the bureaucratized clinic, the great hospital, the multiuniversity. In external affairs the United States found herself in a perpetual cold war, in an arms race against the communist bloc nations, in a morass of brush fire wars and confrontations (the Korean War, the Berlin Airlift, the Indochina War). Her ancient tradition of isolation had ended and the United States was being irresistibly drawn into the vacuum of power left by the decline of the old imperial powers. Meanwhile, the old institutions of socialization (such as the family and, particularly, religion) that had once supplied the orientation which integrated the individual's loyalties were losing their influence. Increasing numbers of persons were turning to social scientists to supply the ideological rationale for man's orientation to the world. It is, perhaps, significant that virtually no one has challenged C. Wright Mills' contention.

> It is now the social scientist's foremost political and intellectual task— for here the two coincide—to make clear the elements of contemporary uneasiness and indifference. It is the central demand made upon him by other cultural workmen—by physical scientists and artists, by the intellectual community in general. It is because of this task and these demands, I believe, that the social sciences are becoming the common denominator of our cultural period, and the sociological imagination our most needed quality of mind.[7]

The tasks that faced social scientists in the immediate postwar period were twofold: (1) to describe the radical reorganization of society and the changed place of the United States in the world and (2) to provide orientation (that is, ideological adaptation) to the changed state of affairs. Few persons at the time were prescient enough to observe that these two tasks were in some measure contradictory. The first belonged to the world of science proper; the second had always in the past belonged to ethics, to politics, to religion, or to social philosophy of a traditional type. One day the ultimate contradiction between these two tasks would have to be confronted.

The unprecedented growth of the social sciences in the immediate postwar period was not due alone to the backlog of students piled up by war service, nor to the G.I. bill which facilitated veteran education, nor to the baby boom, nor even to changes in educational objectives of the social classes which were to bring lower-class and minority students in greater numbers into the universities. The social sciences were enjoying a new prestige as disciplines particularly qualified to analyze the major social changes that were occurring. Moreover, increasing numbers of students turned to the social sciences for the type of orientation Mills emphasized, a type of orientation no longer supplied by their religions. In the colleges and universities the classes of social scientists swelled to overflowing. Everywhere the demand was heard for expanded social science programs. Colleges and universities which had, at best, rudimentary social science programs everywhere increased their staffs and expanded their course offerings. New graduate programs for the training of social scientists were established to supply the need for personnel.

The properties of American society that captured the popular mind in the immediate postwar period were (1) the unprecedented material prosperity that accompanied the transition to a fully constituted mass society (that is, America's character as an affluent society) and (2) the impressive fact that the United States had emerged from World War II as the most powerful nation in the world. In a kind of euphoria most Americans looked upon their society and found it good.

In view of the demand placed upon social scientists to provide explanation and orientation to the changed social order the strong shift of social theory in the postwar period toward holism (that is, the view that society is a transindividual entity in its own right with laws of its own) appears almost inevitable. To be sure, Max Weber, who was widely studied in the United States for the first time in the postwar period, was an elementarist. But Weber had died in 1920 and was not alive to call attention to this fact. Those features of Weber's sociology most useful from a holistic point of view tended to be most exploited. Both Parsons and Mills who had been elementarists before World War II were moving decisively toward holism in the postwar period. Already in the 1930s Sorokin had become a sociocultural holist. If any theory were to emerge in dominant position in the United States in the immediate postwar period it had to be holistic.

Parsons' structure-functionalism became the dominant form of holism in American sociology in the immediate postwar period, because it was better fitted to the milieu than any of its rivals. Sorokin's pessimism disqualified his system of theory for such a role, for in a world euphoric at the material affluence of the mass society and the ego-enhancing concept of the United States as the number one world power, Sorokin was a peddler of global gloom. Mills was already moving toward holism, but he also was emerging as a strident critic of the course of events. Conflict theories, particularly of a Marxian variety, offered holistic interpretations of events. But the intellectual milieu of American social scientists also was responding to the cold war tension between the capitalist and communist blocs of nations. Marxism was a form of holism appropriate to the enemy. To make the case even more decisive, Senator Joseph McCarthy had turned the stereotypes of international communism into a political weapon against all sorts of public figures inside and outside of government who had ever shown sympathy for left-wing ideas or movements.

It was, perhaps, of no little importance for his ultimate standing that Talcott Parsons was located at prestigious Harvard University. Moreover, Parsons, the son of a Congregational minister, brought to his task the work discipline of a monk. His conventional liberalism and programmatic conservativism were brilliantly suited for the task of explaining and vindicating America's status as an affluent mass society and her position as foremost world power. Parsons' qualifications for his self-appointed task were powerfully confirmed by the attempts of Senator Joseph McCarthy to bring his attack upon communist sympathizers and left-wing fellow travelers against Harvard professors and even Talcott Parsons himself. Having thus been authenticated as a legitimate spokesman for the eastern liberal establishment, Parsons' drive for formal rationality and his indefatigable industry could only assure any impartial observer that the task of sociological theorizing was in the best of hands. At this point the very turgidity and opacity of his style became an asset, for the very difficulty of ascertaining the ultimate meaning of Parsons' formulations gave his writings the property of shibboleths that could mean different things to different people. At the inner sanctum of the emerging system of thought was an ever-growing body of writings whose ultimate mystery guaranteed the need for priests of second rank, capable of translating the ideas of the master into a form accessible to the laymen. Parsons had emerged as the sociologists' sociologist, as the high priest of an increasingly decisive system of sociological thought.

Structure-functionalism developed so completely into the status of establishment sociology that toward the end of the 1950s and into the early 1960s some of its exponents claimed that it was coextensive with sociology itself. Under the circumstances C. Wright Mills, who for his part also was moving toward a collectivistic social theory, was automatically cast into the role of the primary anti-establishment sociologist. An ancient dream of sociology, a dream as old as Comte, of the potential of sociology to provide decisive moral integration in a postreligious world significantly lived on in both Parsons and Mills. Talcott Parsons has, perhaps, more completely realized Comte's dream of the sociologist-priest than any other sociologist past or present.

Throughout the period, to be sure, sociologists continued to work in purely empirical contexts and from elementaristic as well as holistic points of view. Always in the background, the powerful example of Max Weber was available for reference. However, as noted above, Weber's sociology was most vigorously exploited in service of functionalistic and systemic arguments. Weber's personal objection to the ideological abuse of social science was largely ignored. When Mills began to elaborate his anti-establishment perspectives, he did not so much bring ideological pretenses to empirical test as to offer alternative ideologies of his own.

It would be pleasant under the circumstances to be able to say that the development of an authentic scientific sociology finally brought the emerging ideological systems to account. However, even in relatively brief retrospect, social events appear to have had more to do with the decline of functionalism than logical criticism or empirical testing.

As the United States moved into the 1960s the cold war continued with all the features a weary public was finding increasingly burdensome: the persistence of a consolidation of power in a relatively small establishment elite; the continuation of the draft; a tendency to maintain an inordinately large part of government business under a cloak of official secrecy; the burdening of the public with the escalating expense of military hardware while domestic programs were short changed; the tendency of the state and war departments to get bogged down in foreign wars and confrontations. Minorities and underprivileged groups began to organize for national action; the Blacks, Chicanos, American Indians and finally women began to organize to press their claims and demand a reordering of national priorities. As the Indochina war deepened, antiwar groups grew more desperate and began to force confrontations with the establishment. The Pentagon Papers case dramatized some of the consequences of official secrecy. The possibilities for abuse resulting from policies that hide political actions under a cloak of secrecy eventually became agonizingly clear in Watergate.

As such sociopolitical events unfolded, it was inevitable that any system of social theory as closely adapted to a limited set of establishment needs as structure-functionalism would be called to account. More and more persons began to challenge what appeared to them to be the latent conservativism of structure-functionalism. As disillusionment deepened the anti-establishment sociology of C. Wright Mills increased in popularity. Ironically, Mills has been more popular after his death. Inevitably, alternatives other than those offered by Mills to establishment sociology have been explored. Conflict sociology has risen in popularity and, as already noted, some structure-functionalists even began to incorporate features of Marxism into the system.

Nor has the exploration of alternatives to structure-functionalism stopped with C. Wright Mills' theories and other forms of conflict theory. Elementaristic theories of many sorts have been opened up for exploration. They include symbolic interactionism, pluralistic behaviorism, phenomenology, ethno-methodology, and existentialism. A forthright, explicitly value-oriented, radical sociology has been advocated. Meanwhile the case for a rigorously empirical scientific sociology has been made. Accompanying this rich ferment of ideas, a new awareness of the possible effect of value commitments on interpretations has sharpened sensibilities. Mutual unmasking of ideological pretenses has occurred.

It is only from a relatively narrow perspective that conceives theory in terms of great quasi-ideological systems of belief, that it can be said that there is, at present, a decline in interest in theory. Rarely has there been more intellectual excitement or more vital conceptual developments on so many fronts at the same time. The new intellectual ferment has been accompanied by scepticism about the claims of personality in the world of ideas and the search for a new principle for the ordering of thought.

Among the developments that have excited many of the younger sociologists in recent years has been the provocative essay by Thomas Kuhn on *The Structure of Scientific Revolutions*. According to his report, Kuhn was impressed by a contrast between the social and natural sciences. While the social sciences were riddled by conflicts and controversies, the natural sciences displayed a mien of outward calm and agreement. While the social sciences seemed to get nowhere, the natural sciences seemed to make steady progress. Kuhn urged that whenever one looked closely at the natural sciences one discovered that things were not always as harmonious as they seemed. Periods of calm alternated with periods of violent disagreement. The notion of "paradigm" supplied the explanation for the phenomenon.

Kuhn defined paradigms as "universally recognized scientific achievements that for a time provide model problems and solutions to a community of practitioners" and also as "accepted examples of actual scientific practice—examples which include law, theory, application and instrumentation together—[which] provide models from which spring particular coherent traditions of scientific research."[8]

According to Kuhn, after a fumbling, controversy-ridden preliminary stage, all of the natural sciences eventually entered upon more stable stages in which unity and coherence were provided by the ordering of scientific practice in terms of paradigms. Scientists whose research is based on a shared paradigm are committed to the same rules and standards of scientific practice. Adherence to a paradigm transforms a group of amateurs into a profession or, at least, into a discipline with specialist societies and claim upon a distinctive place in the curriculums of the colleges and universities. Organized by or in terms of its paradigm a discipline enters upon a period of "normal" science.

> These three classes of problems—determination of significant fact, matching of facts with theory, and the articulation of theory—exhaust, I think, the literature of normal science both empirical and theoretical.[9]

Normal science, according to Kuhn, does not aim at opening up new areas or breaking new ground. It is better described as puzzle solving.

> The scientific enterprise as a whole does from time to time prove useful, open up new territory, display order, and test long-accepted belief. Nevertheless, *the individual* engaged in a normal research problem *is almost never doing any one of these things.* . . . Many of the greatest scientific minds have devoted all of their professional attention to demanding puzzles.[10]

Despite normal science's endeavor to make the world conform to the paradigm, in time anomalies may turn up which resist all efforts at domestication. When many anomalies accumulate scientists may develop an acute sense of insecurity in the presence of their paradigm. In Kuhn's words: "Like artists, creative scientists must occasionally be able to live in a world out of joint."[11]

The sense of crisis that develops with the accumulation of anomalies that do not fit the paradigm may blur, for some individual scientists, its outlines. The social and psychological ground is being prepared for the promulgation of a new paradigm. However, not all individuals are equally ready for such new departures. In Kuhn's words:

> Almost always the men who achieve these fundamental inventions of a new paradigm have been either very young or very new to the field whose paradigm they change. And perhaps that point need not have been made explicit, for obviously these are men who, being little committed by prior practice to the traditional rules of normal science, are particularly likely to see that those rules no longer define a playable game and conceive another set that can replace them.[12]

If the new paradigm is destined to win, the number of persuasive arguments in its favor increase and defections appear in the ranks of adherents of the old paradigm. At some point mass transfers to the new point of view occur as most scientists are converted to the new paradigm. Kuhn quoted with approval Max Planck's observation that a new scientific truth does not triumph by convincing all of its opponents, but because the opponents eventually die and a new generation grows up familiar with it. For the rest "the transfer of allegiance from paradigm to paradigm is a conversion experience that cannot be forced."[13] At least transfer from one paradigm to another cannot be forced in the early stages of the contest between an old and a new paradigm. All this changes eventually as the profession lines up unanimously behind the new paradigm, for "the man who continues to resist after his whole profession has been converted has *ipso facto* ceased to be a scientist."[14]

As Kuhn sees the matter the widespread notion shared by both scientists and nonscientists that science displays a rising line of progress resulting from its rational open-mindedness is an illusion produced by the thought control normal science exercises over its practitioners in the name of its paradigms. He argues that when a scientific community renounces a past paradigm it also repudiates as fit subjects for professional scrutiny most books and articles in which the paradigm had been embodied. As a result of such thought control the average scientist fails to appreciate the revolutionary course that led his discipline to its current position. He accepts the myth that the present position occupied by his discipline is the end point of a rising line of rational progress. Leaving no doubt that his Orwellian vision of science is consciously intended, Kuhn observes: "The member of a mature scientific community is, like the typical character of Orwell's *1984*, the victim of a history rewritten by the powers that be."[15]

The attractiveness of Kuhn's ideas to many of the younger sociologists is not hard to find. In the first place, Kuhn's arguments pander to the sense of inferiority that many social scientists have long experienced in the presence of their natural science colleagues. Kuhn's message first of all is that social scientists need no longer experience embarrassment because of their endless ambiguities, arguments, and controversies. At the very least natural scientists experienced them in the past and will do so again in future revolutionary periods. The presence of so many controversies in the social sciences is merely evidence that they are either in a pre-paradigm or crisis (between paradigms) stage.

Second, Kuhn's arguments are attractive to many social scientists because of his assimilation of science to the models of sociopolitical and religious practices with which social scientists are familiar. Since the eighteenth century natural science and technology have been the primary illustrations of rational development and progress. By contrast the spheres of religion and politics have been characterized by confrontations, coups, and revolutions and in such a perpetual state of crisis that it would be difficult to characterize them as displaying rational progress. And, when the social sciences arose they seemed to display all the traits of the events they proposed to study. However, Kuhn maintains that the difference between natural and social science is illusory. He has found the natural scientists to be routinely engaged in brain washing, thought control, exercising normative authority over routine scientific practice and even controlling the history of the discipline in the interests of the establishment. The development of natural science displays, not rational progress, but revolutionary cycles comparable to those of politics and religion or, perhaps, the cyclical displacement of styles in the arts.

Finally Kuhn's arguments are attractive to some social scientists because of the superficial similarity of some of his key concepts to their own. Kuhn's concept of "paradigm" inevitably conjures up the same term, to be sure with somewhat different meanings, in the social sciences. The term "paradigm" has long been familiar to linguists where, for example, in grammar it referred to the set of all forms containing a particular element, especially the set of the inflected forms of a single root, stem, or theme. Robert K. Merton has popularized the notion that paradigms have an important role in sociology. In his famous paradigm for functional analysis he visualized the paradigm as "a *codification* of those concepts and problems which have been forced upon our attention by critical scrutiny of current research and theory."[16] Also the concept of paradigm as utilized by linguists and as generalized for social science analysis by Merton has many similarities to Max Weber's ideal-type. Weber had suggested that in social science research ideal typical concepts considerably assist in imputation and research. While ideal-types are not hypotheses, or descriptions, or averages, or universal concepts and certainly not stereotypes, they may, Weber argued, be of great value in the development of the conceptual generality and the empirical precision of social science. "An ideal type is formed by the one-sided *accentuation* of one or more points of view and by the synthesis of a great many diffuse, discrete, more or less present and occasionally absent *concrete individual* phenomena, which are arranged according to those one-sidedly emphasized viewpoints into a unified *analytical* construct (*Gedankenbild*)."[17] However a major difference appears between the usage of paradigm by Kuhn on the one hand and by the linguists or Merton and the usage of ideal-type by Weber on the other. The social scientists have employed paradigms and ideal-types to promote description and analysis. Kuhn seems to mean by scientific paradigms total systems of scientific practice which serve to normatively order scientific behavior, that is, Kuhn's paradigms in some respects, close off or limit description and analysis.

The contrast between Kuhn's usage and the traditional social science usage of paradigm (Kuhn's paradigms operate as ethical models in the interest of maintaining the authority of the scientific establishment; the traditional social science paradigms and ideal types were provisional codifications of theory and empirical findings in the interest of extending conceptual analysis or increasing empirical precision) has been obscured by ambiguity in Kuhn's formulations. At no time did he spell out in detail the criteria of scientific paradigms other than to suggest that they were scientific achievements which supply models for the search for problems and solutions of other practitioners or to indicate that a paradigm could include laws, theories, applications, and instrumentation in some sort of ordered package. At times one gets the impression that almost any item in the scientist's repertoire (a law, a theory, even a methodological procedure) can be a paradigm by itself if only it is widely adopted. Or again one gets the impression that only some peculiar total system of scientific practice can qualify as a paradigm.

In his essay on "Power to the Paradigms" Andrew Effrat correctly calls attention to the lack of a clear definition of paradigm. Effrat also compactly summed up the more comprehensive meaning of paradigm that Kuhn at times implies.

> While Kuhn does not provide a particularly clear-cut definition, "paradigm" seems to refer to a theoretical system or perspective that includes: (1) an indication of what are important and researchable questions or problems, (2) general explanatory principles or answers to these questions, (3) "praxis-oriented exemplars" and models for conceptualizing and solving scientific puzzles, (4) criteria for what are appropriate data, methodologies and instruments and (5) an axiology (or value orientations), epistemology and ontology that underlie and ground all of the above.[18]

Conceived in this comprehensive sense "paradigm" becomes a euphemism for a total system of scientific practice whenever this total system operates in a relatively unified and dogmatic manner. But when used in this way, "paradigm" is virtually useless as a tool of scientific analysis for it is a characterization of a total state of affairs which can only be established after the fact.

The very ambiguity of Kuhn's conception of paradigm has been a component in the popularity of the term among the younger social scientists. Since almost anything conceivable can be treated as a paradigm a generation of paradigm finders, analyzers, and inventors has been spawned. Moreover, when paradigm is conceived in its more comprehensive sense it is equivalent to "the official scientific establishment ideology." The exposé of the paradigms thereupon becomes the shortest route to scientific revolution. However, the young social scientists have by no means faced up to the implications of assimilating scientific to religious and political practice as Kuhn appears to have done. If science can no longer be distinguished from religion, an ancient polarity in western thought and experience has collapsed and the once brave battle that rational science fought against total immersion in ideology has been lost.

However, apart from all such unresolved issues, one may well wonder whether the reception by young social scientists of these new ideas may not signify their renunciation of the cult of personality in the world of ideas, their acknowledgement that the age of heroes is over and no longer will their stars illuminate the darkness, for the sun is rising on a new age, perhaps an age of paradigms.

Notes

1. Robert Reinhold, "A Mentor of Sociologists," *ASA Footnotes*, 13 August 1973, p. 3.

2. Edward Shils, "The Calling of Sociology," in *Theories of Society*, ed. Talcott Parsons, Edward Shils, Kaspar D. Naegele, and Jesse R. Pitts (New York: The Free Press, 1961), vol. II, p. 1420.

3. Alvin W. Gouldner, *The Coming Crisis of Western Sociology* (New York: Basic Books, 1970), p. 341.

4. See Gouldner's résumé in *The Coming Crisis*, p. 410.

5. Don Martindale, "Talcott Parsons' Summa Sociologica," *Sociological Quarterly* (Summer 1970), pp. 416–18.

6. Reinhold, *ASA Footnotes*, p. 3.

7. C. Wright Mills, *The Sociological Imagination* (New York: Oxford University Press, 1959), p. 13.

8. Thomas S. Kuhn, *The Structure of Scientific Revolutions* (Chicago: The University of Chicago Press, 1965), pp. x, 10.

9. Ibid. p. 33.

10. Ibid., p. 38.

11. Ibid., p. 79.

12. Ibid., pp. 89–90.

13. Ibid., p. 150.

14. Ibid., p. 158.

15. Ibid., p. 166.

16. Robert K. Merton, *Social Theory and Social Structure*, rev. and enlarged ed. (Glencoe: The Free Press, 1957), p. 50.

17. Max Weber, *On the Methodology of the Social Sciences*, trans. and ed. Edward A. Shils and Henry A. Finch (Glencoe: The Free Press, 1949), p. 90.

18. Andrew Effrat, "Power to the Paradigms," *Sociological Inquiry* 42, nos. 3–4:8. For Kuhn's formulation see *The Structure of Scientific Revolutions*, p. 187.

Selected Bibliography

Effrat, Andrew. "Power to the Paradigms." *Sociological Inquiry* 42, no. 3–4 (1972):3–34.

Gouldner, Alvin W. *The Coming Crisis of Western Sociology.* New York: Basic Books, 1970.

Kuhn, Thomas S. *The Structure of Scientific Revolutions.* Chicago: The University of Chicago Press, 1970.

Mills, C. Wright. *The Sociological Imagination.* New York: Oxford University Press, 1959.

Parsons, Talcott. *Politics and Social Structure.* New York: The Free Press, 1969.

Reinhold, Robert. "A Mentor of Sociologists." *ASA Footnotes* 13 August 1973, p. 3.

Shils, Edward. "The Calling of Sociology." In *Theories of Society.* Edited by Talcott Parsons, Edward Shils, Kaspar D. Naegele, and Jesse R. Pitts. New York: The Free Press, 1961, vol. II, pp. 1405–48.

Sorokin, Pitirim A. *Sociological Theories of Today.* New York: Harper & Row, 1966.

Index